Moral Reasoning

A TEACHING HANDBOOK
FOR ADAPTING KOHLBERG
TO THE
CLASSROOM

RONALD E. GALBRAITH
THOMAS M. JONES

Greenhaven Press Inc. — 1611 Polk St. N.E., Mpls., MN 55413

The dilemma stories in the Handbook, which appear on the gray pages, may be reproduced for classroom use, with the exception of *The Ticket Scheme*, on pages 122-126.

© Copyright 1976 by Greenhaven Press, Inc.

ISBN 0-912616-22-9 Paper Edition
ISBN 0-912616-23-7 Cloth Edition

Dedicated to Kathy, Denine and Deborah.

ACKNOWLEDGMENTS

This handbook represents the culmination of three years of intensive work in translating Lawrence Kohlberg's theory of moral development into various teaching strategies and curriculum materials for teachers. In 1973, the authors produced and tested an experimental version of this handbook. This initial version of a teacher-training handbook was developed under the auspices of the Values Education Project, a joint project involving the Social Studies Curriculum Center of Carnegie-Mellon University and the Laboratory of Human Development of Harvard University. The W. Clement and Jessie V. Stone Foundation sponsored the project directed by Edwin Fenton and Lawrence Kohlberg. Barry K. Beyer, director of teacher training for the Values Education Project, and Edwin Fenton, project director, provided extensive consultation in the preparation of the experimental edition. Frank Alessi and George Westergaard, project staff members, helped to develop the initial teaching process, curriculum materials, and grouping strategies. Anne Colby, Marcus Lieberman, and Betsy Speicher-Dubin, staff members of the Laboratory of Human Development, also provided valuable feedback on the first draft of the handbook.

The authors wish to thank the teachers in the Values Education Project who field-tested the handbook. This group of teachers and their students offered invaluable input which gave direction for subsequent revisions. We are particularly grateful for the assistance of Gerald Clarke of Carnegie-Mellon University and Thomas Wyeth of the Shaler Area School District in Pittsburgh for providing ideas for restructuring the second version of the handbook. Sue Tumpa also deserves a special note of thanks for her good humor and perseverance as she typed the many pages of revision. Finally, we would like to express our gratitude to Barry K. Beyer for his contributions and guidance through each step of this endeavor.

TABLE OF CONTENTS

INTRODUCTION

American educators have struggled with moral education and values for at least a century in the public schools. Some teachers have assumed a cultural mandate to teach a prescribed morality; others have attempted to remove all discussion of morality from the classroom, and still others argue that morality should be viewed as relative. This indoctrination — relativism continuum creates a confusing problem for many educators who wish to help students in this sensitive area. Much of the confusion may come from a misunderstanding of how people learn to cope with social and moral problems.

This Handbook offers a new approach to help educators who desire to systematically consider social and moral issues in a school setting. The approach presented in this Handbook is based on Lawrence Kohlberg's theories about moral development. The Handbook introduces educators to the Kohlberg theory, provides samples of student curriculum materials, and presents a specific teaching process for stimulating moral reasoning. The Handbook is presented in a manner designed to help you experience the key elements in teaching for moral reasoning. The Handbook asks you to consider moral problems that affect educators. You will read and analyze a series of transcripts which highlights certain aspects of the teaching process, the required teaching skills, and the appropriate classroom environment. We have included a series of questions and answers relating to the Kohlberg theory, curriculum materials, and the teaching process.

For more than 15 years, Lawrence Kohlberg, a psychologist, has studied how individuals think about social and moral problems. His studies provide the basis for a helpful advance beyond indoctrination and beyond relativism. Kohlberg began his research with the hypothesis that individuals develop their thinking about moral situations. He began asking individuals to respond to moral problems presented in short stories. He collected data based on their responses. With this longitudinal collection of data, Kohlberg presented a thesis which maintained that human thinking goes through stages of development. Additional testing has allowed Kohlberg and his associates to maintain that these stages of development occur in all cultures. The theory represents a universal explanation of how people develop their thinking about social and moral problems.

Kohlberg's theory involves six stages of moral reasoning, each with a particular perspective on social or moral problems. Briefly, the six stages range from a stage 1 concern for punishment and obedience through a stage 4 emphasis on law and authority to a stage 6 focus on certain moral principles such as justice, empathy, and human dignity. Kohlberg stresses that people are at different stages of moral maturity and that understanding how and why individuals respond differently is vital to education.

Understanding Kohlberg's stages of moral reasoning provides a new direction for moral education. **First**, if educators understand the developmental process, they might create methods to help students reach their full moral maturity. **Second**, the theory contradicts indoctrination. In the past, some educators attempted unsuccessfully to indoctrinate students with certain character traits such as honesty and fairness. As another form of indoctrination, educators might decide to teach the concepts inherent in Kohlberg's higher stages. However, individuals only move through the developmental stages as they personally begin to revise their world view. Therefore, consistently telling students to be honest and attempting to teach the higher Kohlberg stages will not give students sufficient opportunities to test their responses to critical social or moral . problems. The teaching materials and the teaching process described in this Handbook create opportunities for students to examine their own thinking about moral issues as well as the thinking of their peers and other members of society. The problems may never seem completely solved, and the right answers are not the property of the teacher. **Third**, the theory moves beyond relativism. Some educators argue that schools should only provide students with opportunities to state their viewpoints on moral or social problems. In these situations, every student's answer is considered a right answer. Kohlberg maintains that people need to confront and work through many moral problems in an effort to test their thinking. The effort in the classroom should be focused on a continuous search for the best answer to a critical moral problem. **Fourth**, Kohlberg feels that the classroom cannot afford to be value-neutral. Students need to struggle with individual and social values. Students need to examine the social and moral problems of their culture in a systematic and open format.

Certain studies related to Kohlberg's theory of moral development indicate that individuals may develop their moral reasoning by engaging in discussions of moral problems. The teaching process described in this Handbook provides a systematic method derived from the assumption that: students need the opportunity to confront difficult decision-making situations; they need to endorse a position and to think about their reasons for selecting their positions; and they need to hear the reasoning used by others on the same problem.

Lawrence Kohlberg's theory of moral reasoning and the teaching process presented in this Handbook should not be interpreted as an absolute comment on moral education or as **the** trend following all of the other trends in values education. Kohlberg's theory represents a typology, a way of understanding how people think about critical issues of morality. The teaching process represents a blending of many existing teaching skills with an understanding of the theory. Together the theory and the teaching process provide a new direction. Students and the society in which they live can use a new direction, a new method which emphasizes a non-indoctrinating yet systematic examination of social and moral problems. Hopefully, this method can be revised and polished so that it represents much more than a trend or a typology. This last assignment belongs to the classroom teachers who choose to try a new direction with their students.

CHAPTER

KOHLBERG'S THEORY OF MORAL REASONING

Six Stages of Moral Reasoning
A Teacher's Dilemma: The Memo
Some Generalizations About Kohlberg's Theory

SIX STAGES
OF MORAL REASONING

In the late 1950's, Lawrence Kohlberg began to collect data related to moral questions. Kohlberg had studied Jean Piaget's earlier work in cognitive and moral development and used this as a foundation for a 15-year study of moral reasoning. Piaget's work focused primarily on uncovering cognitive stages.[1] Kohlberg's study also focused on a developmental sequence of stages and revealed that individuals restructure their thinking about social and moral questions just as they develop their cognitive structure from the very concrete toward the more abstract.

Specifically, Kohlberg introduced a developmental theory for moral reasoning. The theory presents six stages of moral reasoning:[2]

I. Preconventional Level

At this level the child is responsive to cultural rules and labels of good and bad, right and wrong, but interprets these labels in terms of either the physical or the

[1]As most clearly reflected in thinking, cognition means putting things together, relating events; in cognitive theories, such relating is assumed to be an active connecting process, not a passive connection of events through external association and repetition. [Kohlberg, ''The Concepts of Developmental Psychology as the Central Guide to Education,'' **Proceedings of the Conference on Psychology and the Process of Schooling in the Next Decade**. (Washington: U.S.O.E., 1973), p. 4.]

[2]Kohlberg, Lawrence, ''From Is To Ought: How to Commit the Naturalistic Fallacy and Get Away with It in the Study of Moral Development,'' in **Cognitive Development and Epistemology**, edited by T. Mischel. (New York: 1971), p. 164.

hedonistic consequences of action (punishment, reward, exchange of favors) or in terms of the physical power of those who enunciate the rules and labels. The level is divided into two stages:

Stage 1: The punishment and obedience orientation. The physical consequences of action determine its goodness or badness regardless of the human meaning or value of these consequences. Avoidance of punishment and unquestioning deference to power are valued in their own right, not in terms of respect for an underlying moral order supported by punishment and authority (the latter being Stage 4).

Stage 2: The instrumental relativist orientation. Right action consists of that which instrumentally satisfies one's own needs and occasionally the needs of others. Human relations are viewed in terms like those of the market place. Elements of fairness, reciprocity, and equal sharing are present, but they are always interpreted in a physical or pragmatic way. Reciprocity is a matter of "you scratch my back and I'll scratch yours," not of loyalty, gratitude, or justice.

II. Conventional Level

At this level, maintaining the expectations of the individual's family, group, or nation is perceived as valuable in its own right, regardless of immediate and obvious consequences. The attitude is not only one of conformity to personal expectations and social order, but of loyalty to it, of actively maintaining, supporting, and justifying the order and of identifying with the persons or group involved in it. At this level, there are two stages:

> *Stage 3: The interpersonal concordance of "good boy — nice girl" orientation.* Good behavior is that which pleases or helps and is approved by others. There is much conformity to stereotypical images of what is majority or natural behavior. Behavior is frequently judged by intention. "He means well" becomes important for the first time. One earns approval by being nice.

> *Stage 4: The law and order orientation.* This is orientation toward authority, fixed rules, and the maintenance of the social order. Right behavior consists of doing one's duty, showing respect for authority, and maintaining the given social order for its own sake.

III. Post-Conventional, Autonomous, or Principled Level

At this level, there is a clear effort to define moral values and principles which have validity and application apart from the authority of the groups or persons holding these principles and apart from the individual's own identification with these groups. This level has two stages:

> *Stage 5: The social-contract legalistic orientation,* generally with utilitarian overtones. Right action tends to be defined in terms of general individual rights and in terms of standards which have been

critically examined and agreed upon by the whole society. There is a clear awareness of the relativism of personal values and opinions and a corresponding emphasis upon procedural rules for reaching consensus. Aside from what is constitutionally and democratically agreed upon, the right is a matter of personal values and opinion. The result is an emphasis upon the legal point of view, but with an emphasis upon the possibility of changing law in terms of rational considerations of social utility, (rather than rigidly maintaining it in terms of Stage 4 law and order). Outside the legal realm, free agreement and contract are the binding elements of obligation. This is the official morality of the American government and Constitution.

Stage 6: The universal ethical principle orientation. Right is defined by the decision of conscience in accord with self-chosen ethical principles appealing to logical comprehensiveness, universality, and consistency. These principles are abstract and ethical (the Golden Rule, the categorical imperative) and are not concrete moral rules like the Ten Commandments. At heart, these are universal principles of justice, of the reciprocity and equality of human rights, and of respect for the dignity of human beings as individual persons.

The six stages represent a pattern of thinking which integrates each person's experience and perspective on specific moral issues. Although everyone may be able to memorize certain civic virtues, not everyone will think about important civic issues in the same way or act according to the same "learned" virtue. Therefore, rather than to teach the moral rule related to a specific situation, teachers need to help students examine the reasoning used to solve moral problems. Teachers help students examine their own moral reasoning and the reasoning of others by facilitating discussions of **dilemma situations**.

A discussion of **moral dilemmas** focuses more on the different reasoning used to solve a problem than on the recommended behavior of the central character. Participants who recommend similar behavior frequently have diverse reasons for their recommendations. Examining this diversity has provided the key to Kohlberg's research in moral development. Comments from the discussion of *The Memo* which follows will demonstrate how individuals respond from different stage orientations on Kohlberg's hierarchy.

A TEACHER'S DILEMMA:
THE MEMO

Mrs. Wright, a 12th grade social studies teacher, encouraged the students in her Contemporary American Problems course to become active, responsible citizens and to meet problems head-on. One of the class assignments required students to complete an **Action Module** before the end of the semester. An **Action Module** could involve a number of experiences outside the classroom. For instance, some students spent time riding in a police squad car and visiting the municipal court; other students investigated a recent television editorial concerning the treatment of poverty patients at a community health center. Several students decided to stimulate public awareness of a local transportation issue. Recently, a group of elderly citizens had petitioned the bus company and the city council to issue free passes for the elderly who wished to travel about the city. The students proposed that elderly citizens be permitted to ride buses free of charge and that the city subsidize the bus company.

This group of students conducted a rigorous campaign to uncover the issues involved in the elderly's need for transportation. They formed study groups to investigate the problem; they wrote letters to politicians and businessmen; they even appeared on "The People Speak," a television program featuring local issues. However, the various community leaders ignored the students and refused to discuss the issue.

After two months of frustration, the students

decided to act. The small group of students from Mrs. Wright's social studies class managed to enlist the support of a large number of other high school students and organized a plan to focus public attention on the issue of transportation for the elderly. The first part of the plan involved encouraging all high school students to refuse to ride the designated city buses to school. They urged the students to ask their parents to take them to school. The second part of the plan suggested that masses of students should board the crosstown buses during peak hours. Since all high school students had bus passes which allowed them to ride any city bus, they could use their student passes and monopolize public transportation by filling certain buses and preventing regular customers from using them. The students implemented the boycott/monopolization plan, and it seemed to work well on the first day. The school buses were relatively empty. At the height of the late afternoon rush hour, the bus terminal received reports of crosstown buses filled with laughing and singing students.

The following day Mrs. Wright was informed by the Superintendent that local political leaders would not tolerate the student action. She indicated to the Superintendent that she had cleared the project with the Social Studies Chairman and the school principal at the beginning of the school year and that she was pleased with the way many students had become involved in the community. However, Mrs. Wright received an official memo in her school mailbox the next afternoon:

16

BLOOMSBERRY AREA SCHOOL DISTRICT
H. E. Plandon, Superintendent
Education Building
Bloomsberry, Florida

> TO: Mrs. Helen Wright
> FROM: H. E. Plandon, Superintendent
> DATE: January 18, 1975
> SUBJECT: Recent Student Protest Involving
> Public Transportation

As per our conversation yesterday, you must be aware that the students from your social studies class have organized a most disruptive protest against current public transportation policy. The present situation cannot be tolerated, and you must instruct your students to call off the boycott at once and to refrain from occupying the crosstown buses during peak hours. Your students should be instructed at once (individually and by personal telephone calls if necessary) to drop the issue or risk being expelled from school.

I am sure you will agree that this problem should be handled by the school authorities since it began as a classroom assignment. If the students do not follow your instructions, however, the city authorities are prepared to take appropriate action.

Please make an appointment to see me on Thursday, January 20.

HEP:st

Do you think Mrs. Wright should call the students and cancel the assignment? Read *The Memo* again. Think about the specific circumstances. Consider the issues at stake in the situation. In the space below, take a minute and write two responses. **First**, check ''yes'' or ''no'' in response to the question: ''Should Mrs. Wright call the students and cancel the assignment?'' **Second**, write out **your** reasons why you recommend that particular course of action.

Check one: Yes _____ No _____

Reasons_____

_____

_____

_____

_____

_____

_____

_____

_____

_____

_____

_____

_____

_____

You have expressed your opinion on the problem. Do you think that all the other teachers who read about Mrs. Wright and *The Memo* will respond to these questions in the same way that you have? Do you think that most teachers agree on the appropriate action for Mrs. Wright? Can you imagine a discussion among 30 teachers trying to solve Mrs. Wright's problem?

The following transcript represents a typical discussion of Mrs. Wright's situation by a group of secondary school teachers. As you read through the transcript, you should pay particular attention to the different reasoning used to approach the problem. You may also want to compare your own position and reasons with those expressed in the discussion.

TRANSCRIPT

Jim:
I think Mrs. Wright should call the students and encourage them to call off the protest. The students are interfering with the rights of other people in the community. Besides, a boycott is against the law.

Alice:
A boycott is not against the law! Anyone has a right to influence a change by boycotting a product or a service.

Facilitator:
Alice, do you agree with Jim that Mrs. Wright should comply with the memo?

Alice:
Yes, but the students are not breaking the law. They

19

have a right to protest.

Jim:
But you agree that they shouldn't be allowed to continue?

Alice:
There are other ways of handling the situation. I admire the students' involvement, but I agree that Mrs. Wright should cancel the assignment. She is in a leadership position in the community, and she must consider the welfare of the entire community. She should cooperate with the Superintendent and make every effort to discourage the protest. If she assumes this leadership role, she will be in a better position to get the various factions together to discuss the issue.

Betty:
That will not necessarily put her in a position to get the various groups together. The students will not listen to her if she lets them down on this issue.

Facilitator:
Could you tell us more about that, Betty?

Betty:
Teachers spend half of their time gaining the respect of their students; respect is very important! Mrs. Wright would be unable to face these students again if she cancelled the assignment after telling them to meet problems head-on as responsible citizens.

Jim:
Respect is a very small part of this situation. There are other issues involved here.

Betty:
But not as basic as a student's respect for a teacher.

Jim:
The **law** is not a basic issue in the community?

Todd:
Betty, what about the teacher's respect for the law?

Betty:.
The law is not the central issue here. I still think she must be concerned with the students first. After all, that is her profession.

Facilitator:
Betty, do you think Mrs. Wright has a greater obligation to the students than she does to the law?

Betty:
I don't know. Perhaps.

Dorothy:
I believe there are obligations which rank above the law. I'm not sure about whether the boycott is illegal, but I believe Mrs. Wright should support the students in their action. The students not only have a right to protest a social injustice, but they have a responsibility to help the elderly citizens with their transportation problems. Mrs. Wright should refuse to comply with the memo and should persuade the Superintendent to

support the student action.

Facilitator:
Harvey, you appear upset with the comments concerning Mrs. Wright's decision. Could you respond to the ideas offered so far in the discussion?

Harvey:
Well, I just think that everyone seems very idealistic about a very real situation.

Facilitator:
What do you mean?

Harvey:
Mrs. Wright may not have a choice in the matter. She may **have** to call off the assignment.

Jerry:
How is it that she doesn't have a choice, Harvey?

Harvey:
We don't know if she is tenured or not, right? If she doesn't comply with the memo, she may not have her contract renewed next year. That is reality!

Alice:
You don't see anything else in this situation other than the possibility of her losing a job?

Harvey:
Oh, sure. There are other elements in the situation, but nothing worth losing a job over.

Bill:
Then Mrs. Wright's only concern should be for herself?

Harvey:
Primarily, yes. And that she continue to do a good job in the classroom. She has to think about that.

Betty:
That should provide a great model for the students — always look out for yourself!

Harvey:
Unfortunately, that is the way the world works.

PAUSE

Facilitator:
Does Mrs. Wright have an obligation to the elderly in Bloomsberry? Let me put that another way. From the point of view of an elderly person in Bloomsberry, what is the best thing for Mrs. Wright to do?

Jim:
She should call it off.

Facilitator:
Why, Jim?

Jim:
Because you cannot encourage students to play favorites with the law. After all, the elderly represent only one faction in our society, and this protest is

23

infringing on the rights of other members of the community.

Facilitator:
Harvey, both you and Jim agree that Mrs. Wright should call off the assignment, yet you each mention different reasons. Could you tell us what you think is different about your reasoning?

Harvey:
I mentioned her obligation to herself and her job. Jim talked about an obligation to the law, but we both mean that an individual must make a decision based on what is most important.

Betty:
Yes, but most important to whom? Neither of you seem concerned about the students.

Facilitator:
What about the students? Do you think they might agree that Mrs. Wright should cancel the assignment?

Harvey:
Students might support her if they think she will be fired.

Betty:
The students might support her if they really respect her, but she should not put them in the middle of this situation. She should take a strong stand and lead them through the crisis.

Dorothy:
Support them, yes, but not just for the reason of great rapport. Civil liberties are at stake here. Losing a job is an important issue and a real possibility. If Mrs. Wright is working under that kind of pressure, that, too, is a civil liberties battle. Obviously, these students have touched a nerve in the community, and no one has the right to back away from such an issue.

Jim:
How about the civil liberties of the people who cannot use the buses because of the laughing and singing kids?

Think about the comments made during the discussion. Recall and list several reasons the participants used to defend their positions.

Mrs. Wright **should cancel** the assignment:

1. _____

_____

_____

_____

2. _____

_____

_____

_____

Mrs. Wright **should refuse to cancel** the assignment:

1. _____

_____

_____

_____

2. _____

_____

_____

_____

Write out the most acceptable reason which you heard expressed during the discussion of Mrs. Wright's problem.

_____

_____

_____

_____

_____

_____

_____

_____

_____

_____

_____

DISCUSSION

The transcript represents only a brief segment of a typical discussion involving Mrs. Wright's problem. Some of the participants in the discussion disagreed on the appropriate course of action for Mrs. Wright. Even those who agreed on the action proposed very different reasons for their recommended action. The comments made during the discussion reflect different concerns, different perspectives, and different levels of abstraction. For example, Harvey's major concern revolves around the teacher's need to maintain her job. It seems difficult for Harvey to think about Dorothy's more abstract concept of civil liberties. This discussion reveals that individuals respond differently to a moral dilemma. The reasoning used to solve a dilemma may range from a more self-centered perspective to a more complex perspective involving society's welfare. The reasoning you expressed also falls some place within this range.

The major focus of Kohlberg's studies centers on these varied responses to social and moral problems. Kohlberg **does not** suggest that a particular response represents an indication of one's moral worth. The reasoning which individuals use to solve problems simply indicates how people think about critical moral issues at that time. Kohlberg's research has established a specific, step-by-step pattern of thinking or reasoning through which everyone develops. Everyone initially responds to moral problems from a lower stage of reasoning and slowly progresses through a number of sequential stages. Educators need to

27

become sensitive to this developmental nature of human thinking, especially as it concerns moral thinking. By using dilemma situations with students and by posing appropriate questions, an educator can stimulate students to struggle with social and moral problems. Students who clarify their responses and attempt tentative solutions to such difficult problems may also develop higher levels of thinking.

Comments quoted below are used to illustrate stage-related remarks and should be thought of as **examples only**. The six stages represent general categories of structured thinking concerning moral issues. The stages are not intended as devices with which we categorize one another. An individual rarely responds 100 percent of the time at one stage; however, the thinking involved concerning a specific moral issue will probably represent a particular stage orientation. Although we can roughly analyze Harvey's remarks as predominantly pre-conventional, stage 1 or 2, it would be necessary to explore a number of moral dilemmas and moral issues with Harvey in order to analyze his modal stage — the stage most frequently used to respond to diverse dilemma situations. The cognitive developmental approach is premised on the notion that stage 1 reasoning lays the foundation and is a prerequisite for stage 2, which in turn lays the foundation and is a prerequisite for stage 3, and so on. In this fashion, individuals restructure their thinking about moral issues by using their existing stage of reasoning and slowly incorporating elements of the next higher stage. For example, each individual in the discussion of *The Memo* related to the issues from his or her predominant stage of moral reasoning:

Harvey:
We don't know if she is tenured or not, right? If she doesn't comply with the memo, she may not have her contract renewed next year. That is reality.

Oh, sure, there are other elements in the situation, but nothing worth losing a job over.

Students might support her if they think she will be fired.

Harvey's prevailing concern about Mrs. Wright's job, whether or not she is tenured, and whether the students will support her if they know she might lose her job, reflects a pre-conventional, stage 1 or 2 mode of reasoning.

Alice:
She is in a leadership position in the community, and she must consider the welfare of the entire community. She should cooperate with the Superintendent and make every effort to discourage the protest. If she assumes this leadership role, she will be in a better position to get the various factions together to discuss the issue.

Betty:
That will not necessarily put her in a position to get the various groups together. The students will not listen to her if she lets them down in this issue.

Mrs. Wright would be unable to face these students again if she cancelled the assignment after telling them to meet problems head-on as responsible citizens.

Although Alice and Betty disagree on the action Mrs. Wright should take, they share a primary concern which revolves around their desire to please and help others and avoid letting them down in this situation. Betty's remarks reflect her strong commitment to a relationship with the students.

Alice, however, has extended her concern toward a commitment to the entire community, a stage 4 orientation, yet she indicates a strong need for approval from others. Alice's reasoning may reflect a transitional mode between stages 3 and 4.

Jim:
I think Mrs. Wright should call the students and encourage them to call off the protest. The students are interfering with the rights of other people in the community. Besides, a boycott is against the law.

The **law** is not a basic issue in the community?

You cannot encourage students to play favorites with the law. After all, the elderly represent only one faction in our society, and this protest is infringing on the rights of other members of the community.

Obviously, Jim's concern focuses entirely on one's obligation to respond within the letter of the law. Although he discusses the rights of all individuals within the community, his reasons revolve around the stage 4 need to maintain the existing rules and social order.

Dorothy:

I believe there are obligations which rank above the law. I'm not sure about whether the boycott is illegal, but I believe Mrs. Wright should support the students in their action. The students not only have a right to protest a social injustice, but they have a responsibility to help the elderly citizens with their transportation problems.

Losing a job is an important issue and a real possibility. If Mrs. Wright is working under that kind of pressure, that, too, is a civil liberties battle. Obviously, these students have touched a nerve in the community, and no one has the right to back away from such an issue.

Dorothy's comments include an understanding of Harvey's concern about employment, of Betty's comments on rapport, and of Jim's consideration of the legal implications. However, Dorothy's reasoning reflects a more complex understanding of the various roles and issues involved in Mrs. Wright's dilemma. Dorothy sees issues beyond the legal realm, and she recognizes responsibilities to all of the characters in the situation. Dorothy's perspective requires a capacity to role-take or empathize with each character. Her post-conventional, stage 5, perspective also includes consideration of all the possible issues at stake. She can even interpret Harvey's concern for Mrs. Wright's job as a civil liberties issue rather than merely the possibility of unemployment.

SOME GENERALIZATIONS ABOUT KOHLBERG'S THEORY

Kohlberg derived these stages of moral reasoning empirically from longitudinal studies in the United States. The stage theory has also been validated in cross-cultural studies and other related research programs during the past decade. In association with Lawrence Kohlberg, a diverse group of educators and psychologists have further refined the theory through 15 years of research concerning the way individuals reason about moral problems. The following generalizations represent some of the results of that research:

1. *The stages are cross cultural:* In cross cultural studies involving middle class urban males in the United States, Taiwan, and Mexico, and lower class peasants living in villages in Turkey and Yucatan, the results confirmed the developmental theory. Despite divergent cultural, social, and religious backgrounds, the subjects moved through the same stages of moral development in the same sequence. While the rate of movement varied between cultures, the basic concept of universal stages of moral development emerged clearly.

2. *Movement through the stages progresses through an invariant sequence, and stages cannot be skipped:* The evidence suggests that individuals develop through the same sequence of stages. The attainment of a higher stage will always have been preceded by the attainment of all lower stages. Since each stage presupposes the reasoning of each and

every previous stage, it is not possible to skip stages of development. For example, stage 1 and 2 reasoning must be incorporated into a stage 3 mode of thinking; and, therefore, an individual cannot jump from a stage 2 to a stage 4 orientation.

3. *Development occurs because of an attraction to the next higher stage of reasoning:* An individual has the capacity to comprehend reasoning presented at the next higher stage of development. Since the reasoning may appear more logical and comprehensive and, therefore, more adequate in the face of a dilemma situation, individuals may be attracted to the next stage of reasoning. This does not mean that the higher stage is always adopted or even verbalized, but that the listener may begin to incorporate elements of the higher stage in future solutions to moral problems. This constant reconsideration and restructuring of moral reasoning provides the basic elements of the developmental theory.

4. *There are individual differences in the rate of moral development and in the highest level of moral maturity attained:* Although children and adolescents move at varying rates of speed through the stages, pre-adolescents move through the pre-conventional level, adolescents usually achieve the conventional level and adults move toward the post-conventional level of reasoning. However, individuals can become frozen at any level. Actually, less than 20 percent of the adult population reasons at the post-conventional level. Stage 4, the law and order orientation, is always the most common stage, and it

is possible for adults to reason at the lower stages of moral development.

5. *The stages are not a set of cultural beliefs taught to children:* An analysis of the moral development theory, especially as it is related to a teaching process, indicates that the stages do not represent a set of moral maxims which can be taught to children by adults. The stages represent abstractions which children (and later adults) develop on their own as their intelligence matures and they attempt to cope in a consistent way with dilemmas that arise and arguments they hear. Research by Leary (1972) indicates that didactic presentation of moral dilemmas has little or no effect on the developmental level of the students' thinking.

6. *Moral maturity increases a person's ability to resolve moral conflicts:* With maturity the individual is able to empathize with a greater number of individuals in various dilemma situations. At the higher levels of moral development, more perspectives are taken into account in reasoning about moral conflicts.

7. *Moral reasoning is related to behavior:* Although additional evidence must be collected to further support this generalization, some research indicates that mature moral judgment is displayed by individuals who also act in genuinely moral ways. Some limited research related to student activism and obedience indicates a correlation between action and the particular stage orientation of the subject.

8. *Moral development can be stimulated in the classroom:* The research of Kohlberg and his colleagues has also established that students who participate regularly in discussions of moral dilemmas often begin to articulate reasoning at higher stages of development. Specifically, the discussions promote some change or maturity in the nature of moral reasoning for some of the participants. The discussions which promote the most change involve participants at different, but adjacent, stages. Therefore, active discussion among participants at different stages seems to promote change.

These generalizations provide a direction for a new, non-indoctrinating form of moral education. Moral growth is determined by an individual's awareness of perspectives beyond the immediate self. Moral growth represents an ability to see the other side and to focus on the great issues. In order to grow morally, individuals need the opportunity to role-take the parts of others in dilemma situations. Individuals, especially students, need the opportunity to engage in discussions of social and moral problems. Participants in these discussions need to have an opportunity to present their own reasoning and to listen to the opinions of others.

This understanding of the Kohlberg theory of moral reasoning implies a specific teaching strategy for stimulating moral development. A discussion of a moral dilemma should provide students with the following opportunities:

a. To consider genuine moral problems.

b. To experience genuine social and cognitive conflict during a discussion of a moral problem.

c. To apply their current level of thought to problematic situations.

d. To be exposed to the next higher level of thought.

e. To confront their own inconsistencies in reasoning over a variety of moral issues without someone stressing a right or wrong answer.

Curriculum materials featuring dilemma stories are designed to confront students with genuine moral problems. Creating a situation where students disagree over the appropriate action for a central character promotes genuine social and cognitive conflict. The class discussion which focuses on **reasons** for recommending a particular course of action provides students with the opportunity to apply their current level of thinking. An active discussion among students also creates the setting for exposure to higher levels of moral reasoning. Finally, asking students to work through a number of social and moral problems throughout their educational experience provides an opportunity for them to confront some of their inconsistencies in reasoning.

CHAPTER

THE DILEMMA
STORY

Essential Ingredients
A Dilemma Story: "Hey, Sam, the Truck Is Here"

The method used most frequently to confront students with genuine social or moral situations involves the use of a moral dilemma. A moral dilemma story may be presented through a reading, a film, role-playing, or other media. The dilemmas may emerge from at least three sources: the specific content of the course, current issues in contemporary society, and dilemma situations related directly to the lives of the students.

ESSENTIAL INGREDIENTS

A dilemma story includes five essential ingredients:

1. **Focus:** The situation in the dilemma should focus on the lives of the students, the course content, or contemporary society. The dilemma should be considered genuine.

2. **Central Character:** The dilemma should involve a central character or primary group of characters around which the dilemma remains focused. Students make moral judgments about what the central characters should do.

3. **Choice:** The story or situation must involve a choice for the central character. The character in the dilemma should have two action alternatives which present a definite conflict. Neither action choice should represent a culturally approved ''right'' answer. In the dilemma *The Memo*, Mrs. Wright had to choose between complying with the request of her supervisor or supporting her students in their involvement with a community issue. Mrs. Wright

certainly felt the social norms which pulled her in two directions and created conflict for her. Each dilemma story must include a genuine conflict for the main character.

4. **Moral Issues:** Moral dilemmas revolve around key moral issues. Kohlberg identifies some of these issues:

Social Norms	Property
Civil Liberties	Roles and Issues of
Life	Acceptance
Sex	Authority
Personal Conscience	Punishment
Contract	Truth

The Memo , for example, involves the issues of authority, personal conscience, affectional roles, civil liberties, and possibly contract. Participants in a discussion may choose to focus on any one issue in a dilemma, and the teacher/facilitator should be prepared to ask appropriate questions related to each moral issue in a story.

5. **A "Should" Question:** Each moral dilemma ends with a specific question which asks about what the character **should** do in the situation. Asking the "should" question keeps the discussion centered on moral judgments in a dilemma. If, however, you ask participants to respond to what Mrs. Wright **would** do in the situation, you are asking them to predict what she might do. Before individuals are willing to predict the action in a given situation, they often want every possible detail concerning the central character and the possible courses of action.

Students are also reluctant to answer the question: What **would** you do in this situation? Again, before anyone is willing to share their prediction of their own behavior, they want to be certain that they have the "right answer." Anyone, however, can share his thoughts on what another person **should** do in a difficult situation.

A discussion of what someone **would** do, although often interesting and sometimes relevant to moral considerations, often promotes an exercise in psychology rather than morality.

Only after the participants have discussed what **should** be done is it helpful to discuss the possible disparity between what one **should** do and what one **would** do. For example, in a 7th grade social studies class, the students spent nearly an hour debating whether or not a character in a dilemma story **should** use a copy of an important exam (which he found in a school trash barrel) to help study for the upcoming test. Although the students did not agree on what action the character **should** take and they had diverse reasons for defending a course of action, they eventually focused on the potential difference between what a person **should** do — the "right" thing to do — and what a person might actually do in such a situation. In this case, the discussion of the **should** and the **would** responses can be extremely helpful in providing students with an opportunity to examine possible inconsistencies between their own moral judgments and moral action. In the following story which is designed for students, look for the five essential ingredients of a dilemma.

A DILEMMA STORY: "HEY, SAM, THE TRUCK IS HERE"

The mines have been closed for almost six weeks now because of the strike. The first two or three weeks were not so bad. Everyone who works in a mine and belongs to a union expects an occasional strike and always allows for such things. Families store extra food and build up small savings accounts. The union provides some food and a small supplemental pay allowance for striking workers. Now, however, cupboards are empty and savings are gone — even the union funds are available only for miners with over 15 years of service. Children take smaller lunches to school, and family meals consist of soup and day-old bread.

Sam Lentoli manages the only large grocery store in the small mining community. Sam worked in the mines for over 25 years and knows the terrible conditions and the safety hazards which the union is protesting. He is thankful that he can keep his family going and his youngest daughter in college with his income from managing the store. His wife is glad that Sam does not have to go into that black hole ever again.

Sam has just answered the phone for the sixth time that evening. He continues to receive call after call from old friends and other miners in the community asking him about the possibility of credit at the store. Sam is deeply troubled. The owner of the store also owns at least half of the stock in the mining company and is eager for the strike to end. He has instructed Sam that no credit will be extended to striking mine workers — under any conditions.

The next day Sam receives two calls early in the morning. The first from the store owner: ''Sam, I hear people have been asking you for credit at the store. I know that you sympathize with the union and the workers, and this puts you in a tough spot. Let me make it easier for you — if you break the non-credit policy, you can look for a job back in the mines!'' The second call comes from an old friend and a union organizer in the mines: ''Sam, the people have to get credit at your store. You can provide these people with some food, Sam. I will make sure the store is repaid after the strike is settled. I am sending a truck down to pick up a load of groceries to distribute to 30 families. It should be there by 9:30. I can have another truck there this afternoon.''

Should Sam fill the order when the truck arrives?

3

CHAPTER

THE TEACHING PLAN

THREE PARTS
OF A TEACHING PLAN

Part I: The Original Dilemma

The first part of the Teaching Plan for a moral dilemma includes general guidelines for beginning the class discussion. After the initial clarification of the facts and terms in the story, the teacher should determine the amount of disagreement over the choice of action of the central character. Moral dilemmas should create genuine conflicts for individuals. Although Kohlberg's theory implies that students need to focus on the different **reasons** for recommending a particular course of action, a good dilemma story should also produce a difference of opinion concerning the action. If students disagree over the action position, they will be more inclined to discuss the reasons for their different recommendations. For example, students will readily discuss the moral issues involved in Sam's situation if they initially disagree over whether or not he should fill the order when the truck arrives. Each Teaching Plan includes an instruction concerning disagreement on the action position.

Part II: Alternative Dilemmas

Since the students will have more of an investment in the discusison if they initially experience some conflict concerning the action question, a series of alterations for the original dilemma serves to increase the conflict in the story. The alterations may increase the conflict by either focusing more specifically on one of the moral issues in the story or by dramatizing one of the conflicting social norms in the dilemma. For example, if most of the students in the class agree that Sam should fill the order, a teacher could present the alteration of the story which indicates that Sam may face criminal charges for helping the miners take property which does not belong to them. The alteration emphasizes the issue of punishment and could cause some of the students to decide that Sam should not fill the order. This, of course, sets up a discussion of the reasons for some people changing their initial position on action because the punishment issue was introduced. A teacher could also introduce an alteration which specified that Sam is severely disabled and may not be able to find another job if he is fired from the store. This alteration dramatizes one of the social norms which are in conflict for Sam (his obligation to maintain his job as opposed to his obligation of friendship for the other miners).

As long as the class disagrees about the action questions with at least a 70-30 split, it should not be necessary to use one of the alternative dilemmas. However, the alterations to the original story may be used as additional topics of discussion after the class explores the dilemma story. A teacher may choose to use the punishment alteration later in the discussion if the students do not mention that particular consideration.

Part III: Probe Questions

A teacher who facilitates a discussion of a moral dilemma has two primary tasks: promoting student interaction and making certain that the discussion remains focused on the moral issues of the story. In order to accomplish these two objectives, a teacher can employ different kinds of questioning techniques. Certain interaction or perception checking questions help to promote interaction among the class members:

"Do you agree with what Harvey just said about the dilemma story, Betty?"

"Would someone summarize the reasons which have just been given for Sam refusing to fill the order?"

"Would you respond to Dorothy's comments about civil liberties?"

"Terry, you disagreed earlier with Jane's position concerning Sam. Could you paraphrase her position and respond to her from your point of view?"

These questions should help to encourage students to talk to each other about the dilemma. Teachers should also use a more specific type of question to focus the discussion on the moral issues of the dilemma. Probing questions are presented as the third part of the Teaching Plan to help accomplish this objective. Issue-related probes, role-switch probes, and universal consequence probes all help to stimulate discussion of the moral aspects of the dilemma story.

Issue-related probes: Many of the probe questions included in the Teaching Plans are designed to focus on particular moral issues within the dilemma story.

Does Mrs. Wright have an obligation to obey the Superintendent's directive? Why or why not?

Does Mrs. Wright have an obligation to the students in her class?

Should Mrs. Wright comply with the memo if it means that she will run the risk of being fired?

Does Sam have any obligation to the striking mine workers? Why or why not?

Does Sam have any obligation to the store owner? Why or why not?

The probe questions listed above focus on the issues of obligation and punishment. You may use an issue-related probe question in at least two ways. **First**, students may initiate a discussion of a particular issue such as punishment. When this happens, a teacher may choose to sharpen the focus on the issue by using a probe question which places the dilemma character in direct contact with the issue: "What if Sam knows that he will be in trouble with the authorities?" This type of probe question is especially useful when the students have merely mentioned the issue, but have not clearly recognized it as an important consideration in the story. **Second**, students may remain involved in a discussion of a moral dilemma and not perceive a particular issue. An issue-related probe question may move the general class discussion to an examination of a specific moral issue.

Role-switch probes: The major portion of a discussion of a moral dilemma revolves around what the central character in the story should do. After the students discuss their reasons from the point of view of the central character, a role-switch question encourages them to consider their reasoning from the point of view of another character. Role-switch probe questions are especially helpful in giving students an opportunity to see the other side of the issue or situation, to expand their perspectives on complex social and moral situations.

From the point of view of a parent in the district, should Mrs. Wright cancel the assignment? Why?

From the point of view of an elderly person in Bloomsberry, should Mrs. Wright cancel the assignment?

Why do you think that the store owner might not want Sam to fill the food order for the miners?

From the point of view of another customer at the store, should Sam fill the food order for the striking miners? Why or why not?

Role-switch probes can be especially useful in checking the consistency of reasoning and examining the changes in reasoning in the same dilemma story. For example, students may decide that Sam should fill the food order for the striking mine workers because he would want somebody to help him out if he were on strike. When they are asked to consider the question from the point of view of the store owner, however, they may decide that the store owner has a right to protect his store and to use his business to force the miners back to work. Such contrast in reasoning concerning the same dilemma story provides an excellent opportunity to examine the difference between helping friends and obeying one's employer. A more general probe question could pursue this difference: "Which do you think is more important, helping some friends who may be committing a crime or obeying the directions of your employer? Why?" Role-switch probes may often provide students with the opportunity to respond to the dilemma from their highest stage of reasoning.

Universal consequence probes: Usually near the end of a discussion, the teacher may introduce questions which consider the consequences of the reasoning which has been examined.

Should students have the same rights as other citizens?

Should you always protest inequities which you find in a society, even if it means breaking the law?

Should someone always/never help a friend who asks you to do something which violates a rule?

Should a person who disobeys a rule or law always be punished if he is caught?

Considering the universal consequences helps students think about the implication of their reasoning for the society as a whole. These questions, asked in an open, non-indoctrinating manner, should suggest to students that their thinking about important social and moral problems affects all of society. Probe questions, both those presented in the Teaching Plan and those which teachers make up during the discussion, serve several important functions. The right probe question can serve to stimulate a lagging discussion. A probe question can also focus the discussion on important moral issues and generate thinking about the greater issues and social perspectives involved in a dilemma story.

The probe questions should be studied by the teacher prior to the class discussion and should be used at the appropriate time in the class. One of the most important skills of a teacher/facilitator is knowing when to use the appropriate question which will promote student interaction or focus on some important aspect of the dilemma story. The list of probe questions in each Teaching Plan should be interpreted as a guide only. It is not always necessary to use all of the probes. Use a probe question when it will serve a specific objective. The most general kinds of probes involve the use of the questions: "Why is that important to you?" "Could you tell us a little more about your reason?" and "What is the most important reason the main character must consider in making his decision?"

TEACHING PLAN: "HEY, SAM, THE TRUCK IS HERE"

Part I: Hey, Sam, the Truck Is Here"

Distribute class handout, "*Hey, Sam, The Truck Is Here*" which describes Sam and the miners. Make sure that the students understand the terminology in the dilemma and can state the nature of the dilemma which Sam faces.

Determine by a show of hands or in some other way how the class feels about whether Sam should fill the order for the miners.

If the class divides with at least one-third of the students on each side of the issue, choose one of the small group strategies listed on pp. 85-90. Proceed with the discussion, skipping the alternative dilemmas.

Part II: Alternative Dilemmas

If the class agrees that Sam SHOULD fill the order, one of the following alternative dilemmas can be used to provoke disagreement.

A. The owner calls Sam again. He tells Sam that if he helps people take property which does not belong to them, he will not only be fired but he will have charges brought against him. Should Sam fill the order?

B. If Sam is severely disabled and unable to work in the mines if he lost his job at the store, should he fill the order?

If the class agrees that Sam SHOULD NOT fill the order, one of the following alternative dilemmas can be used to provoke disagreement.

A. Sam receives another phone call. Someone says that some of the striking miners plan to start stealing food if they cannot get it any other way. Should Sam fill the order and prevent the possibility of stealing?

B. A young mother comes into the store and tells Sam that the food situation is so bad that some people are planning to send their children to live with relatives in another county. Should Sam try to prevent this by filling the order?

Part III: Probe Questions

1. Does Sam have any obligation to the striking miners? Why or why not?

2. Does Sam have any obligation to the store owner? Why or why not?

3. Is the owner of the store right in forbidding credit for the hungry miners? Why or why not?

4. Should Sam's friend put Sam on the spot with his request for a truck full of food? Why or why not?

5. Should the miners be striking? Why or why not?

6. Should some government agency give families who are on strike enough food so that they will not be hungry? Why or why not?

TEACHING PLAN: THE MEMO

Part I: The Original Dilemma

Have the participants read *The Memo*. Make sure the participants know the basic facts and conditions described in the dilemma. You might ask, "What has happened to Mrs. Wright and the students in her social studies class?"

Determine how the participants divide on the issue of whether Mrs. Wright should call her students and withdraw the assignment?

If the class divides with at least one-third of the class on each side of the issue, choose a Small Group Strategy listed on pp. 85-90 and proceed with the discussion.

If there is too little disagreement over the issue, proceed to the alternative dilemmas below. These dilemmas should help to produce more disagreement and enhance discussion.

Part II: Alternative Dilemmas

If most of the participants agree that Mrs. Wright SHOULD call the students, use one of the following alterations:

A. Several parents and a state senator called Mrs. Wright. They told her that they believed in what she had done and would support her. They encouraged her not to call off the assignment.

53

B. Mrs. Wright had agreed with her students that she would not interfere with their attempts to become involved in some community issue.

If most of the participants agree that Mrs. Wright SHOULD NOT call the students, use one of the following alterations:

A. Mrs. Wright was a non-tenured teacher. The local Teachers' Association told her that it could not support her if the Superintendent suggested that her contract might not be renewed.

B. Mr. Hotchkamp, a lawyer representing the Over-Sixty Association, called Mrs. Wright and asked her to withdraw the assignment and discourage the students. He indicated that the students' actions could interfere with current negotiations between the city council and the Association.

C. Mrs. Wright was informed that the bus company planned to revoke all student passes if the protest continued.

When the participants disagree on action after discussing one of these alterations, choose a small group strategy listed on pp. 85-90 and proceed with the discussion.

Part III: Probe Questions

Use the following questions at the appropriate time to facilitate the discussion:

1. From the point of view of a 62-year old individual living on a small fixed income, what should Mrs. Wright do? Why?

2. Does Mrs. Wright have an obligation to support the students in her class who are carrying out the Action Module assignment? What is it?

3. Does she have an obligation to obey the Superintendent's directive? Why or why not?

4. From the point of view of a parent in the district, should Mrs. Wright withdraw the assignment? Why or why not?

5. What should be the most important consideration for Mrs. Wright when she responds to the memo? Why is it an important consideration?

6. Which is more important — her role as a citizen or her role as a teacher in this situation? Why?

7. Should teachers be allowed to give assignments which call for student involvement in community affairs? Why or why not?

8. Do the students have an obligation to protest the inequities of public transportation in Bloomsberry? Why or why not?

9. Does the Superintendent have an obligation to the students involved in the protest? What is it?

10. Should students have the same rights as other

citizens? Why or why not?

11. Should the schools be organized to promote in-
    dividual freedom and responsibility for the welfare
    of others? Do you think the Bloomsberry Area
    School District promotes responsible citizenship?
    Why or why not?

   To lead a moral dilemma discussion, a teacher
should have a confident grasp of the Teaching Process
as well as a familiarity with the particular dilemma
story. The next section of the Handbook includes a
step-by-step guide for facilitating a classroom discussion of a moral problem. Throughout the outline of
the steps in the Teaching Process, you should note the
coordination between the overall process and the
specific Teaching Plan.

CHAPTER

THE TEACHING
PROCESS

Step 1. Confronting a Dilemma
Step 2. Stating a Tentative Position
Step 3. Examining the Reasoning
Step 4. Reflecting on an Individual Position

In teaching for moral development the teacher takes the class through a four-step Teaching Process.

For this Teaching Process to be most effective, three other elements of meaningful discussion must be considered: teacher role, student role, and classroom atmosphere.

STUDENT ROLE

Review the transcript of the discussion involving *The Memo*. In this case, the teachers participated as students in the discussion. You should be able to determine some of the characteristics of the student role. The following words may reflect their role during the discussion of Mrs. Wright's dilemma:

> listening
> defending an individual position
> questioning
> probing
> empathizing
> arguing
> tolerating
> thinking
> responding to questions

In the discussion transcribed the participants spend most of the time talking to one another, not to the facilitator. They question each other, defend their own positions, and respond to questions from the facilitator who also fulfills a particular role.

TEACHER ROLE

What kind of leadership or direction did the teacher/facilitator provide during the transcribed discussion? Did the facilitator ever impose an individual position or mode of reasoning on the group? What words would you use to describe the teacher's role during the discussion?

Educators who have observed a similar discussion of a moral dilemma volunteered the following list of words and phrases which characterize the teacher's role during such a discussion:

> task-giver
> group leader
> moves the discussion
> quiet much of the time
> flexible, yet directive
> tolerant
> restrained
> questioner
> listener
> open to all ideas
> did not have "the answer"
> summarizer
> clarified ideas
> informal
> sincere

Notice the kinds of questions which the facilitator asks:

"Alice, do you agree with Jim?"

"Could you tell us more about that, Betty?"

"Betty, do you think that Mrs. Wright has a greater obligation to the students than she does to the law?"

"Harvey, both you and Jim agree that Mrs. Wright should call off the assignment, yet you each mention different reasons for your position. Could you tell us what you think is different about your reasoning?"

The questions are non-threatening and do not promote a closed answer. Each question attempts to promote an increased focus on the problem and a greater degree of student-to-student interaction. The teacher/facilitator should not be the major contributor to a discussion of a social or moral problem; however, the teacher does need to guide the discussion and assume responsibility for keeping the exchange of ideas focused on the problem.

CLASSROOM ATMOSPHERE

The lists of words which reflect the teacher and student roles during a discussion of a moral dilemma also suggest the necessary climate of the classroom. This particular approach for analyzing social and moral problems depends on a setting which promotes both free-flowing discussion and specific, guided inquiry. The development of more mature moral reasoning occurs primarily because students have the opportunity to examine their own reasoning in the light of reasons given by others in the discussion. Since the research indicates that higher stage arguments may appear more logical and consistent to individuals operating below that particular stage, the atmosphere of the classroom should encourage students to speak freely and to listen intently. Observers of a class discussion of a moral dilemma have used the following words to characterize the classroom atmosphere:

> open
> debate-like
> lively
> student oriented
> loud
> sometimes aggressive
> frustrating - no clear answer
> informal
> task oriented
> thought provoking
> unsettling
> stimulating
> sincere
> problem-centered
> involved

Your role in setting the appropriate classroom climate cannot be stressed enough. The students need to believe that you are genuinely interested in them and that you would like to help them make sense out of some puzzling problems. If you can communicate the fact that you have no intention of forcing truths upon them or of packing your values into their minds, then you have a head start on the most productive classroom climate.

THE TEACHING PROCESS

Teaching for moral development requires the

teacher to assume the role of a facilitator in a group discussion. In order to demonstrate that a discussion goes through certain phases, the teaching process has been divided into specific steps. Teachers should go through four steps in teaching a moral dilemma:

Step 1: Confront a Moral Dilemma. Teachers should provide students the opportunity to confront a moral dilemma. Teachers present the dilemma story, make sure that students can state the circumstances in the story, make sure that all appropriate terminology is defined, and make certain that the students understand the problem which faces the central character.

Step 2: State a Tentative Position. Teachers should give students the opportunity to state a tentative position on the moral dilemma. **First**, students need time to think about where they stand on the moral issues involved in the story. **Second**, they need a chance to take an individual position on the dilemma, often by writing down their position and their reasons for supporting it. **Third**, teachers need to determine how the total group stands on the moral dilemma. This may be accomplished by a show of hands or some other voting technique which will indicate whether or not some genuine conflict concerning the appropriate action for the central character exists in the group. A teacher may even want to give some students a chance to express their reasons for assuming certain positions on the dilemma; this would help indicate to the group that different individual positions exist on the dilemma story.

Step 3: Examine the Reasoning. Next, teachers should select appropriate deployment strategies and introduce appropriate questions which will promote maximum student discussion of the moral issues in the story. A variety of small group settings often provides the best environment for the students to begin exchanging ideas on the decision facing the central character. The small groups help to insure that everyone gets a chance to express his reasoning and provide an excellent warm-up for the large class discussion. After a period of time devoted to small group discussions, teachers should next facilitate a discussion involving the entire class. After the students have an opportunity to exchange reasons in the small groups, they need to participate in a larger discussion where the facilitator can help guide the discussion of the dilemma.

Step 4: Reflect on an Individual Position. During the final phase of the class discussion, the teacher should help students reflect once again on their positions concerning the dilemma. Students may be asked to summarize the reasoning which they have heard during the discussion or to state their positions after they have heard all of the other opinions offered by the rest of the class. Although some students may indicate that they have changed their thinking during the discussion, the objective is not to form a consensus or to try to reach a conclusion regarding the appropriate action for the dilemma character. The process remains open-ended, and the students should be encouraged to continue thinking about their own positions and the comments which they have heard in the group discussion.

The diagram on the following page represents the four steps in the teaching process and the various sub-steps. The four **squares** down the center of the diagram symbolize the **major steps in the process and the activities which the teacher should initiate**. The **circles** forming the extensions of each square represent **sub-steps or specific activities** which are usually student-centered.

THE TEACHING PROCESS

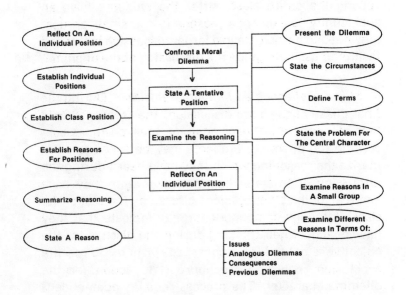

STEP 1

CONFRONTING A MORAL DILEMMA

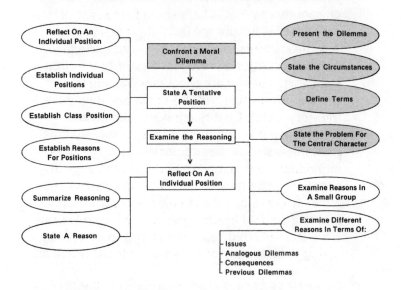

A. **PRESENT THE DILEMMA:** A dilemma story may
be presented in a variety of ways. *The Memo* was
presented as a printed handout for the teachers to
read prior to the discussion. Role-playing, a segment of film, a newspaper clipping, or an audio-tape
are alternative methods of presenting dilemmas to a
class. Using a variety of media helps students see
that moral dilemmas do not always come from
printed material within their curriculum. The
primary objective is to present students with a
central character who faces a difficult social or moral
problem.

B. **STATE THE CIRCUMSTANCES:** Before students can seriously discuss the moral issues involved in a story, they must understand and describe the circumstances of the situation. Who are the characters in the story, and what is their relationship to one another? What is happening to the central character? What are the facts of the story?

Ask the students to answer the questions in their own words. After one student describes the circumstances, the others are encouraged to add their comments and observations to the restatement of the story's plot. Continue this translation and clarification process until you feel certain that the class understands the circumstances of the story. Individuals cannot make moral judgments about a situation which they do not really understand. This initial discussion of the circumstances will help to promote student involvement and will demonstrate to the students that you are sincerely interested in having them search for the answers to the problem.

C. **DEFINE TERMS:** Defining terms is similar to clarifying the circumstances. Students must understand all aspects of the dilemma story in order to take an individual position and offer reasoning on the problem. For example, a participant in the discussion of *The Memo* who does not understand the term boycott would be at a serious disadvantage. Teachers should review each dilemma story and attempt to identify the terms which may be difficult for their students. Students should, whenever possible, define the terms.

D. STATE THE PROBLEM FOR THE CENTRAL

CHARACTER: The last step in helping the students to confront a dilemma involves a clear statement of the problem facing the central character. For example, if the class believes that *"Hey, Sam, The Truck Is Here"* concerns whether the mine workers should be on strike, they do not understand the problem for the central character. They will not be able to respond to the issues concerning the order of the store owner and the subsequent decision of Sam. Someone in the class should be able to summarize Sam's problem: "Sam must decide whether to allow his friends to have the food from the store." Or "Sam has to decide between his obligation to his friends and his obligation to the owner of the store." The following transcript represents a typical dis-cussion of *"Hey, Sam, The Truck Is Here."* This segment follows the class through the first step, *Confronting a Dilemma.* As you read through the transcript, identify the various sub-steps.

NOTE: The following transcript represents an example of a teacher using a moral dilemma story in a social studies class. This particular class was involved with a unit in American History dealing with the development of organized labor.

Teacher:
Good morning. In the past few days, our class has examined some of the conditions which resulted. in the development of labor unions in the United States. What are some of the ideas which really stood out in your mind as we examined the material related to labor history?

Anne:
We learned that in some factories and mines the workers had very bad conditions.

Teacher:
What do you mean by bad conditions?

Anne:
Well, the miners worked long hours and were not paid very much.

Dory:
Some people even got seriously hurt while they were working.

Teacher:
What about the communities where these laborers worked?

Paul:
The conditions were bad there, too.

Anne:
Yeah, like the lousy housing and the fact that they never had any money.

Bill:
The mining towns even had stores where the workers bought all of their food.

Denine:
But haven't they been trying to start the union to change some of this?

Maggie:
Yeah. The miners tried to get the workers to band together to protest safety problems, low pay, and long hours.

Bill:
They protested by going on strike.

Teacher:
How many of you know somebody — a relative or a neighbor — who belongs to a labor union of some kind?

Most of the students raise their hands to indicate that they know someone who belongs to a labor organization.

O.K. How many of you know someone who has gone out on strike as part of a union protest?

About half of the students raise their hands.

What is it like when someone is on strike?

PAUSE

How do families get along when the husband or wife is not working?

Sue:
They don't have much money and cannot buy food and stuff.

Paul:
They have to use their savings!

69

Ravennah:
What if they don't have any savings?

Paul:
I remember reading about the Pullman strike. The union decided to put part of the union dues into a fund to help workers in case they called another strike.

Sue:
So the union has some savings which they use!

Teacher:
Do you think families have a rough time during a strike?

Ravennah:
Yes, because the workers don't get their full pay.

Teacher:
O.K. Let's look at a story about a group of people in a community who are in the middle of a strike.

The teacher passes out copies of "Hey,Sam, The Truck Is Here."

Take a minute and read the story. Think about all of the characters in the story and what the problem seems to be.

The students read through the story.

Could someone tell us in your own words what is happening in this story?

Debbi:
A guy named Sam works in a store, a grocery store, which sells things to the workers who are out on strike.

Paul:
He's the manager!

Cathy:
Sam used to work in the mines, so he is a friend of some of the strikers.

Ravennah:
The workers are not getting money any more from the union.

Sarah:
Their families are hungry!

Teacher:
Whose families?

Sarah:
The strikers.

Dory:
Yeah, the kids had to take smaller lunches.

PAUSE

Teacher:
Are there any other characters in the story? Sam and certain strikers have been mentioned. Is anyone else involved?

David:
Sam's boss — he owns the store.

Bill:
And he told Sam not to give credit to the striking mine workers.

Teacher:
Why do you think he will not give credit?

PAUSE

Anne:
Because he also owns the mine.

Bill:
He only owns half of it.

Anne:
But he wants the strike ended. That's why he won't give any more credit.

Teacher:
Why do the strikers need credit anyway?

David:
Because they are not getting supplemental pay.

Teacher:
Who knows what "supplemental pay allowance" means?

Sarah:
Isn't that the money which unions save to use in case of

strikes? This strike has lasted so long they are running out.

Teacher:
O.K. Some workers refer to this as their supplemental pay.

The story also refers to the black hole. What do you think that refers to?

Paul:
The mine!

Teacher:
But why call it a black hole?

Anne:
Because it probably isn't great to work down there. The story says that is the reason why they are striking in the first place.

Teacher:
Thank you, Anne. Remember the article we discussed which stated that more lives were lost in mining accidents than in any other occupation?

PAUSE

Teacher:
O.K. Let's list on the chalkboard the different characters involved in the story.

The students review the list of characters as the teacher lists them on the board.

Bill:
We forgot about Sam's daughter. He is trying to put her through college.

Teacher:
Why is it important for us to be aware of Sam's daughter?

Maggie:
Because Sam needs to keep his job.

Teacher:
Well, what is Sam's problem in this story?

PAUSE

Sue:
Sam is put in the middle!

Teacher:
Sue, what do you mean about Sam being in the middle?

Sue:
Well, his friends want him — or expect him — to give them food on credit, and the owner told him he had better not give credit.

Cathy:
The owner told Sam to find another job if he gives credit to the strikers.

Doug:
Yeah, and the truck is coming and Sam better make up his mind.

NOTE: Discuss the four sub-steps in the preceding transcript.

STEP 2

STATING A TENTATIVE POSITION

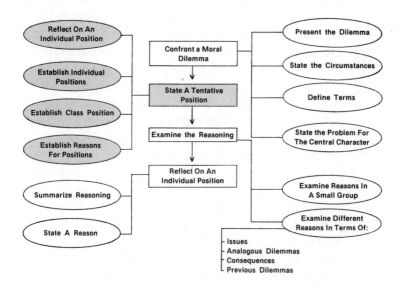

A. **REFLECT ON AN INDIVIDUAL POSITION:** After students confront a dilemma story, they need an opportunity to think about the final question. Once the circumstances of the story are clearly understood, a moment of silence may promote serious, individual reflection on the action question: ''Should Sam fill the food order when the truck arrives?''

B. **ESTABLISH INDIVIDUAL POSITIONS:** After everyone has an opportunity to think about the action question, additional time should be provided to establish the individual position on action and to indicate a reason for the position. You may want to ask students to use 3 x 5 cards or the back of the dilemma handout to write down two responses: 1) An initial ''yes'' or ''no'' response to the action question and, 2) a personal reason for answering yes or no. Writing out the responses privately avoids the common conflict of peer pressure which can persuade some students to respond in a particular manner. This time for private reflection and response represents an important preparation for the class discussion. Students need time to think about their own reasoning prior to hearing a variety of other reasons. After all, the rest of the class period will be devoted to an exploration of the various responses to the dilemma story. If students seriously prepare their own response to the dilemma, they will be able to present and defend their own positions and listen to other positions. The teacher should stress the tentative nature of this initial response. Anyone can later change his position and his reasoning and adopt additional elements of the discussion into his own thinking.

C. **ESTABLISH CLASS POSITION:** After helping students establish their individual positions on the action a character in a dilemma story should take, you need to determine the different responses among the entire class. Determining the amount of disagreement over the central character's action helps you find out whether conflicting opinions exist which will serve to promote discussion. You may ask students for this public declaration of their positions by using a variety of voting methods:

1) Ask students to indicate their positions by a show of hands. Three possible positions can be taken — yes, no, and undecided. You may also ask students to close their eyes for this method if you feel that peer pressure helps to determine positions in your class.

2) A variation of the hand raising method involves asking students for a "thumbs up," "thumbs down," or an "arms folded" (undecided) response to the dilemma question. A good discussion of a moral dilemma depends on an initial disagreement among class members regarding what a character should or should not do. You should determine the approximate division in your class so you can decide whether to pursue a discussion of the original dilemma or pose an alternative dilemma to the class. Once you establish that students disagree over the appropriate action, you have the class primed for the next step — discussion of reasons for assuming such a position on the action question: "Should Sam fill the food order when the truck arrives?"

D. **ESTABLISH THE REASONS FOR INDIVIDUAL POSITIONS:** After determining that members of the class disagree about the appropriate action, you should help students begin stating some of their reasons for making the decision. Spend a few minutes asking different people in the class to volunteer their reasoning related to the dilemma story. Listing a variety of reasons on the chalkboard or merely mentioning a variety of reasons which individuals have recorded during their initial reflecting period will help prepare students for the small group discussion and will also indicate to the students that people have many different reasons for recommending a particular action position.

NOTE: Do not abandon the original dilemma too quickly even if there is no clear division on the appropriate action. Take a few minutes to explore the reasoning which students have even if they agree on the initial action position. Then, if no division develops, proceed to an alternative dilemma in the teaching plan.

The class discussion of *"Hey, Sam, The Truck Is Here"* continues below and represents the second step, **Stating a Tentative Position**, of the Teaching Process.

Teacher:
I would like each of you to take a minute and think about Sam's situation. You should consider all the circumstances and the various implications for the different characters in the story.

PAUSE

Please take one of the 3 x 5 cards which I have placed on the tables, and write down two things. First, indicate with a "yes" or a "no" what you think Sam should do. "Yes," if you think that Sam should fill the order when the truck arrives; and "no," if you think he should not. Make these responses privately — you will have a chance to see how other people decided later! Second, write out your **reason** for taking that position. That is, why do you think Sam should or should not fill the order. Two things on the card: yes or no to the dilemma question and why you support this position.

Jerry:
What if you just don't know?

Teacher:
What do you mean, Jerry?

Jerry:
Well, I can't decide.

Teacher:
O.K. Try to take a position if possible. Try to determine which position you feel strongest about. If that is not possible and you are truly undecided, write the following on your card: first, an indication of your decision with a question mark rather than a ''yes'' or ''no''; second, at least two questions which you would like to have answered to help you make up your mind. Anyone else who is really undecided may follow the same procedure.

The students spend several minutes writing their responses on the cards.

Teacher:
Has everyone had a chance to complete the card? I need to find out how much the class agrees or disagrees on what Sam should do. We should be able to determine that with a show of hands. If you have written on your card that Sam **should** fill the food order when the truck arrives, raise your hand.

Twenty students raise their hands.

Teacher:
O.K. How many people indicated on the card that Sam **should not** fill the order?

Five students raise their hands.

Are there some who cannot decide one way or the other?

Jerry and one other student raise their hands.

Sue:
See, almost everyone says that you should help your friends.

Teacher:
Why is that? What are some of the reasons you have written down for recommending that Sam should help his friends by filling the food order?

Diana:
Because you should help out your friends.

Teacher:
Why is that so important?

Diana:
Friends are important. People don't have that many friends, and besides, these people are hungry.

Teacher:
Well, what if the owner of the store calls Sam just

before the truck arrives and tells him that if he helps people take property which does not belong to them, he will not only be fired but he will have charges brought against him. What do you think Sam should do?

PAUSE

Take a minute to think about this new situation. All the same circumstances except that the owner calls Sam again with this new remark.

The teacher waits, but several students indicate that they want to respond.

Teacher:
O.K. Several people want to comment on this new dimension of the story, but first I want to find out something. How many of you now think that Sam should fill the order? Please raise your hand.

Fifteen students raise their hands.

How many still feel that he should not?

Eleven students raise their hands.

And, undecided?

Jerry raises his hand.

Teacher:
O.K. There are many aspects of this situation to think about. I would like you to spend some time in smaller groups where you will have the chance to discuss your position and your thoughts concerning Sam, the store owner, and the striking workers.

STEP 3

EXAMINING THE REASONING

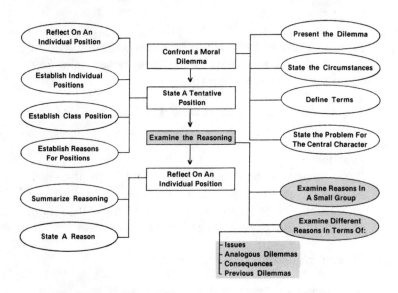

A. EXAMINE THE REASONS IN SMALL GROUPS:

Before the entire class begins to discuss the dilemma story, students need a chance to meet in smaller groups to examine their reasons for endorsing a specific action position. A small group meeting insures that each individual has an opportunity to share his or her own thinking with a few other class members. This time spent prior to the more wide-open class discussion allows the group to think about the different reasons for each particular position and to test one another's ability to defend a position.

Setting Up Small Groups

Kohlberg's theory suggests that students need to hear reasoning at the next higher stage for moral development to occur. The approach to using Kohlberg's theory described in this Handbook assumes that in any individual class, students operate at adjacent stages of moral development. Therefore, small groups working together on tasks that focus on reasoning maximizes the chance for students to hear other points of view concerning a particular issue. In the small groups, students work on tasks that require them to clarify, define, and listen to reasons for a particular position. In addition to these objectives which relate directly to moral development, working in small groups helps students to achieve a number of other objectives that relate to learning skills and self-concept. Work in small groups helps students accomplish a specific task, to develop listening skills, and to be willing to accept a variety of ideas.

Teachers who do not presently use small group deployments in their classrooms need to think about some additional areas of concern. Students need to be socialized to small group activities. Teachers should select tasks geared to the sophistication and abilities of their students. As a general rule of thumb, small group activities should start with a relatively simple task such as listing all the reasons of the members of the group and selecting the best two reasons from that list. After students have demonstrated a capability for completing simple tasks, it is appropriate to move to more complex tasks such as role-taking or preparing for a debate. The ability of students to work in small groups depends on the expertise of the teacher. The teacher can do a number of things to help make group work a successful experience:

1. Assign clearly defined tasks that relate to the dilemma and take into account the capabilities of the students. Task cards which state the specific goals for group work help groups to focus on the assigned task.

2. As you move from group to group, enter the groups without disrupting the discussion. A teacher should enter a group as a listener and make appropriate decisions based on how well the group is working to complete the assigned task. Appropriate actions for teachers include asking probing type questions, asking summarizing or interaction type questions, and assigning additional meaningful tasks that will help the group prepare for the full class discussion.

3. Small group work requires the acceptance of a higher than usual noise level in the room. Teachers should often step back and scan the entire class to get a picture of how the class is working in a small group setting.

4. Teachers should make an effort to vary experiences and small group tasks from lesson to lesson.

5. Teachers may find it helpful to record some of the discussion that takes place in the small groups for

use in the full class discussions. This can improve the transition from small group to full class discussion.

In general, teachers should use a variety of grouping strategies based on the ability of the students and/or the nature of the dilemma. Small group work has a direct carry-over to other classroom activities, and group work in the regular curriculum will reinforce the quality of the moral development lesson.

Small Group Strategies

Strategy A [*Homogeneous grouping*]

Deployment: Divide the class into groups of five to eight students. Each group should consist of individuals who agree about the appropriate action on a dilemma.

Student Task: Have each group make out a list of reasons for holding the position that it does. After the groups have worked for a period of time on this initial task, have them select the two best reasons which they think reflect the best defense of their position on the moral dilemma.

Teacher Notes: You should move from group to group helping each group develop their list of reasons, if necessary. After approximately 15 minutes of group work, ask the recorder from each group to report on the final list of best reasons. Since you will have several groups working on listing reasons for opposing positions on the moral dilemma, a general class discussion focused on moral reasoning should follow the reporting of the groups. Encourage students to challenge one another's reasoning and help focus the dialogue on why individuals believe one reason is more appropriate than another. The discussion will often focus on two or three conflicting reasons. If the general class discussion becomes too repetitive or loses momentum, use a probe question or an alternative dilemma to refocus the discussion or to check the consistency of those students arguing a particular position. Frequently ask students who are not active in the discussion to summarize the dialogue or offer their opinion of the discussion.

Strategy B [Heterogeneous Grouping]

Deployment: Organize the class into small groups with each group including members who **do not** agree about the action of the dilemma. For example, in this strategy a group might include two to three individuals who think Sam should fill the order, three to four who think he should not fill it, and a student who cannot decide.

Student Task: Ask students in the mixed groups to discuss their positions and the reasons for their positions in order to produce a list containing the two best reasons (according to the group) why Sam should fill the order, and the two best reasons why Sam should not.

Teacher Notes: One of the objectives of this strategy is

to have students discuss the dilemma from each position on action with the task of the group focused on reasoning rather than on the initial position. A general class discussion should follow group reports. With this strategy you may find it helpful to have groups record their best reasons on the chalkboard so that everyone can see the different ways of thinking about the dilemma.

Strategy C

Deployment: After determining a class division on action , divide the class into groups of five to eight students whose members agree about the appropriate action on a dilemma.

Student Task: Have members of each group share their reasons for holding the positions they do. Give each group five to ten minutes to exchange the reasons. Each student should write down the reasons mentioned in the group.

Teacher Notes: The teacher should move from group to group listening to the discussion. Next, reorganize the groups so that half of a group holding one position exchanges places with half of a group which stated an opposing position on action. Have the members of the new groups (now mixed) complete the following tasks:

1. Report to the other half of the group their reasons developed in the previous discussion.

2. Discuss the reasons. Specifically, each half of the new group should challenge the reasons offered by the other half and ask questions about why they think their reasons are good.

3. Each half of the new group then meets for three to five minutes and decides which reason the other half offered which seems most appropriate. They decide about the reasoning they have heard the other half of the group offer — not the reason they necessarily agree with. For example, the three students who believe Sam should fill the order will try to agree on the best (most acceptable **to them**) reason which they have heard from the group which believes that Sam should not fill the food order for his friends, the mine workers.

4. The groups report their decision to the class with specific emphasis on why each sub-group selected a particular reason which others had offered.

   You may want to prepare a group task sheet which explains the small group task for this strategy. Allow sufficient time for the groups to complete the tasks. This strategy emphasizes the analysis of the reasoning used by individuals who recommend an opposing action position.

Strategy D

Deployment: After some class discussion of the dilemma and the reasons for certain individual positions, divide the class into groups of five to eight students.

Student Task: Ask each group member to assume a particular role in the dilemma and to consider, from that character's perspective, what the central character in the dilemma should do and why.

Teacher Notes: After the group meeting, members of each group may represent their character in a central dialogue concerning the dilemma. The discussion should remain on why a character believes a particular action is right. This strategy is especially useful in helping students think about the dilemma story from different perspectives and different roles.

Strategy E

If your students do not disagree on the action position of a dilemma story (even after you use the alternative dilemmas provided in the Teaching Plan), you may want to use a strategy which by-passes the decision on action and emphasizes different reasons. continues

Deployment: Divide the class into four groups.

Student Task: Ask two of the groups to assume the "yes" position on the dilemma question and the other two groups to assume the "no" position. Ask the groups to think of all the different reasons a person might give for responding either "yes" or "no" to the question.

Teacher Notes: After giving the groups sufficient time to brainstorm a list of reasons, ask the groups to help you develop (on the chalkboard) a list of reasons under each action category. Once you have a variety of reasons listed, you can ask the class to indicate which reason is most acceptable to them as a rationale for pursuing a specific course of action. You may even ask them to rank order the reasons listed. When someone selects one reason over the others, ask him to discuss why it is more acceptable. This should begin a discussion of moral reasoning.

The Undecided Students

These recommended strategies often call for arranging the class according to individual positions on the action question. Students who remain undecided about the action decision may participate in a variety of ways:

- Undecided students may join any group with the explicit responsibility of listening to the discussion and asking questions about reasons for particular positions.

- The undecided students could also form a separate group to develop a list of questions which they would like to have answered by the other groups to help them reach a decision.

- Undecided students could record the various reasons given during a class discussion and select what they think reflects the best reasons given for each action position.

B. EXAMINE DIFFERENT REASONS IN TERMS OF: ISSUES, ANALOGOUS DILEMMAS, CONSEQUENCES, AND PREVIOUS DILEMMAS:

As the discussion moves from the small groups to the entire class, the dilemma story may be analyzed in terms of:

Issues: Each social or moral problem involves a number of specific moral issues. The best method of focusing on a particular issue is to use one of the probe questions provided in the Teaching Plan. You should try to introduce an issue-related probe question in a way that does not disrupt the natural flow of the student discussion. Introduce an issue-related probe either as the students begin to talk about a particular issue or when the discussion seems to lag and the issue has not yet been examined. For example, if your students have not discussed whether Sam has an obligation to the owner of the store, you might introduce the probe: "Does Sam have an obligation to the store owner? Why or why not?"

Analogous Dilemmas: An analogous dilemma is any story or situation which relates directly to the dilemma under examination. The analogous dilemma is similar in terms or circumstances and involves the same moral issues. Students may present analogous dilemmas; you may think of analogous situations which are more meaningful to the lives or experiences of the students; or you may find material from a local newspaper or magazine which presents a dilemma situation analogous to a story which you and the class have examined. If a class appears to have difficulty analyzing a particular dilemma, you may think of an analogous dilemma to help promote a more productive class discussion. For example, a class of ninth-grade students considering the case of Walter Hickel could not become really involved in the discussion of whether he should have resigned his cabinet position as Secretary of the Interior because he did not believe in all the activities of the Nixon Administration. The teacher introduced another situation involving a high school student who had been appointed treasurer of the Student Council only to discover that other members of the Council had planned a social activity which would intentionally discriminate against certain groups in the school. ''Should the student resign the position rather than be a part of the plan?'' The students began a very lively discussion of the issues related to that analogous situation.

Consequences: Many discussions of social and moral problems usually include some consideration of the consequences of someone's action. You may choose to begin a discussion by asking the students to examine the consequences related to either course of action presented in the dilemma story. Listing some of the consequences and their impact on certain characters in the dilemma may provide a useful, intermediate step prior to asking students to take an action position and indicate reasoning. Thinking in terms of consequences should also help students begin to consider additional perspectives and roles in each situation. The focus of the discussion, however, should remain on the reasoning for a particular position and not on the "right" decision based on fear of moral consequences.

Previous Dilemmas: As you confront students with a number of moral problems during the course of a school year, many of the stories will involve identical issues. You may find students responding with inconsistent reasoning concerning similar situations or issues. This is not uncommon, and it provides an opportunity to help the student consider the possible inconsistency of his reasoning on certain moral issues. Attempting to resolve inconsistencies and struggling with the same moral issues as they appear in different situations can facilitate moral development. The teacher should point out these inconsistencies in an open, non-threatening and non-judgmental way and ask the student to consider them. For example, a teacher could say, "Todd, I remember that you told us several weeks ago that a person should never do anything to hurt a friend because that same friend could help you out some time. Now you say that Sam should think about the store owner and all the things he could lose by giving credit to the striking mine workers. Could you tell us something about how or why you have changed your mind?" Todd's apparent inconsistency does not indicate that he is not responding seriously to the discussion of the problem, but that he is struggling with new perspectives regarding certain issues. Research indicates that often when people seem inconsistent in their reasoning (known as "disequilibrium"), they may experience their greatest growth in moral maturity. The following transcript continues through the third step of the teaching process:

Teacher:
I would like the 11 people who indicated that they think Sam should not fill the order to break into two groups and meet on this side of the room. I would like the 15 or so people who think he should fill the order to break into 3 groups and move some chairs around over by the windows to form your groups. Jerry, would you spend some time in a "yes" group and a "no" group and take some informal notes on what's going on, what reasons people are giving for the opposing views. Then, perhaps, we can start our large discussion with your personal summary of what you heard going on in those groups.

Now, each small group will have about 10 minutes to complete the following task: First, give everyone a chance to share his reason for saying that Sam should or shouldn't give credit to these striking workers. Second, see if you can agree on a best, most acceptable reason for that particular action. And, third, come up with a very good question which your group would like to pose to one of the other groups who took the other position. O.K., move to your groups.

Diana:
Wait a minute, are we still including that last thing you added about the store owner threatening to have Sam thrown in jail?

Teacher:
Yes, the story is the same with my added dimension that the store owner tells Sam that he will have him

arrested if he fills the order.

Students move to various groups with a great deal of noise and comment about where Jerry will go to listen and how Sam probably should have stayed in the mines. The movement into small groups is usually accompanied by a degree of levity about the dilemma situation. The transcript will focus on two of the small groups:

Group #1

Maggie:
What are we supposed to do?

Marc:
Tell each other why we think Sam should not fill the order when the truck arrives.

Dave:
Then everyone here is a "no"!

Sue:
We also have to pick the best reason and write some questions to ask during a later discussion, and we only have 10 minutes.

Maggie:
Well, I'll go first. I don't think Sam should fill the order because he could lose his job and his daughter would have to drop out of school.

Debbi:
Yeah, his first loyalty is to his family and not to the striking union.

Sue:
Besides, the owner has helped Sam and Sam shouldn't break the trust that the owner has placed in him.

Dave:
There is another reason that I think is important. What if he gets caught and the owner turns Sam in to the police. Then he won't be of any value to the owner, his family, or the men on strike.

The teacher approaches the group and sits on the periphery listening to the discussion.

Maggie:
Well, what's the best reason?

PAUSE

Dave:
We haven't heard Marc's reason yet.

Marc:
I agree with Sue. Sam shouldn't break the trust the owner has in him.

Debbi:
I still think Sam should think of his family first. After all, he had spent 25 years in the mines to better his family's position in life. Why should he risk all that for the miners?

Sue:
If the mine workers are such good friends, they shouldn't put Sam in such a tough situation. Good friends don't do things like that to each other.

Maggie:
I hadn't though of that. Let's use Sue's as our best reason when we talk with the other people.

The teacher moves to another group.

Group #2

Denine:
Well, like I said, Sam was in the mines once and he probably was on strike, too. He knows how these people feel and if he can help them out, it's his duty. If he doesn't, who will?

Sarah:
Wouldn't someone else like the government or something bring food to this community? Sam should not get stuck with all the blame.

Bill:
Nobody is blaming him. He just happens to be in a position to help his friends. Besides, the government can't go around feeding everyone who goes on strike.

Ravennah:
Yes, but the government should help those people out.

Bill:
Look, how could Sam go on living in that town and

facing all of those people if he didn't help them get food? It's not like he is a criminal or something — he's just helping his friends.

PAUSE

The teacher has been listening to the group discussion.

Teacher:
You seem to be focusing on Sam's obligation to his friends. Even when I added the part about the owner pressing charges, you didn't change your position, did you?

The students shake their heads, "No."

Teacher:
Do you think Sam has an obligation to the owner of the store?

Sarah:
Not like he does to his friends!

Teacher:
Tell us more about that, Sarah.

Denine:
Wait a minute, Sarah. Sam owes the store owner something. After all, he trusts Sam with running the store.

Sarah:
Well, maybe, but Sam's friends are counting on him.

Denine:
And the owner is counting on him to protect the store.

Joe:
Yeah, and the owner is going to throw Sam in jail —
that's not friendly!

The group laughs at Joe's sudden comment.

Teacher:
Wait a minute. Joe just made me think of something.
Does the owner of the store have the right to tell Sam
not to give credit?

PAUSE

Bill:
Sure he does! It's his store and his food.

Teacher:
So, if I agree to take care of something of yours and
you give me specific instructions not to loan it out, do I
have an obligation to follow your wishes?

Bill:
Yeah.

Denine:
That's different.

Teacher:
How?

Denine:
In the story people are hungry!

Teacher:
So Sam has the right to give away the owner's food?

Ravennah:
No, he doesn't.

Teacher:
Why?

Ravennah:
Well, maybe it is an issue of property.

Teacher:
Now you're saying he should not fill the order,
Ravennah?

Ravennah:
I don't know. The people shouldn't have to go hungry,
but the store owner should not have to lose his food.

Teacher:
O.K., you have about two minutes left to work in this
small group. I want to go listen to another group. Think
about the issues you have discussed, and be ready to
tell everyone else the best reason for Sam to fill the
order. Or if some of you have changed your thinking at
all, make a note to yourself about what you heard to
change your mind, and be ready to share that with all of
us.

*The teacher asks the small groups to turn their desks
around so that they can see one another. The students
form an approximate circle with their desks in order to
begin a discussion involving the whole class.*

Teacher:
Jerry, you were sitting in on several groups. What
kinds of reasons were discussed in the various groups

concerning what Sam should do?

Jerry:

The people who said Sam should not fill the order argued that Sam's first loyalty was to his family. They also said that if he gave the supplies, he would break a trust that had developed with the store owner. The "yes" group mentioned that Sam's first concern should be his friends who were on strike.

Teacher:

Jerry, which of these reasons did you find most attractive?

Jerry:

I'm still undecided. He has an obligation to help the strikers, but not if he's going to risk the loss of his job and possibly get arrested. Sam would want to help his friends, but also wouldn't want to go to jail. I just don't know.

Teacher:

Do you have any thoughts on what Sam should do, Jerry?

Jerry:

I think he should try to help the strikers, but he shouldn't get himself in trouble with the store owner.

Paul:

But Jerry, you can't do both those things. He either has to help his friends or he has to stand by the store owner.

Teacher:

I heard a number of students in the small groups discussing Sam's obligations. Would someone like to explain to whom Sam has the greatest obligation?

Tom:
Sam should think about himself first.

Dory:
No, what if all the workers back in the Pullman strike had only looked out for themselves? This labor movement would never have gotten off the ground.

Sarah:
That's true, but it's more than just trying to keep the union together. Our group talked about Sam's obligation to his friends.

Joe:
Yeah, maybe Sam worked alongside some of these people in the mines, and they are good friends. You can't turn your back on good friends when they need you.

Teacher:
Why is that so important? What if Sam was one of the striking workers and knew the man who managed the store?

Dave:
Do you mean you should sacrifice your family to help your friends? The store owner would expect help from the manager if his family was going hungry.

Teacher:
Which obligation is more important? Sam's obligation to help his friends or his obligation to his family?

Sarah:
It's more than just giving help or expecting someone to help you. Good friends trust one another. Just like when Sam worked in the mines. You trusted people who worked next to you to help you out when times were difficult. Sam shouldn't let those people down.

Debbi:
Do you mean you would sacrifice your family to help your friends?

Ravennah:
How would he be sacrificing his family?

Debbi:
His daughter would have to drop out of college. He would not be able to support the rest of his family.

Teacher:
We have been discussing Sam's obligation to his family and his friends. Let's think about another issue. What obligation does Sam have to protect the property of the store owner?

At this point the students center their discussion on Sam's obligation to the store owner. During the discussion a student does mention the fact that the store owner owns a large stock in the mine and begins to question the store owner's right to force the strikers back to work by refusing credit. One student suggests a solution to Sam's problem.

Paul:
The store owner knows that the strikers plan to ask Sam to fill their orders on credit. So, the store owner could

close the store and call the police and this would stop Sam from giving away the food.

Maggie:
If that happens, those strikers should just break into the store and take the food they need to survive.

Teacher:
Do you think the strikers should do that?

Bill:
No, because the store owner has a right to do what he wants to with his store.

Denine:
But not if people are starving.

Ravennah:
That's right. Human lives are more important than property.

Teacher:
The issue of property rights and human life seems to be important. I've heard some of you talking in small groups about which is more important. Now Todd has mentioned it again. Let's focus on the conflict of property rights and human life. Would someone respond to Todd's idea that human life is more important than property rights?

NOTE: Students begin to discuss the importance of property rights and human life as they relate to Sam's situation. The students bring up important main ideas. The teacher helps provide some organization for the discussion by listing on the chalkboard some of the students' thoughts concerning the importance of property rights and human life.

STEP 4

REFLECTING ON AN
INDIVIDUAL POSITION

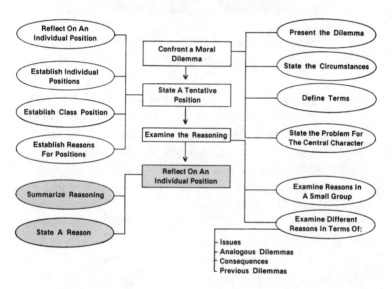

The last phase of a class discussion should emphasize another period of reflection for each individual. Hopefully, students will not close the door on the discussion as they leave the room. The positions which you have asked them to take have been tentative, and the reasoning which they have shared should be open to continued analysis. Therefore, the last step includes some additional time set aside for a summary of the reasons offered during the discussion and an opportunity to state an individual reason once again.

A. SUMMARIZE REASONING: Several methods can be used to promote a summary of the reasons discussed in the class.

1. Ask the students to think about the reasons given by those holding the opposite action position. For example, "If you believe that Sam should fill the food order, what is the best reason which you have heard suggesting that he should not?"

2. Ask the students to recall the many reasons given during the discussion. Record these on the chalkboard. Next, ask the students to agree on a rank order for the list of reasons. (Which one is most acceptable, second best, etc.) You will probably have two lists to match the different action positions. This task serves as a summary technique and also promotes further discussion of the moral problem.

B. STATE A REASON: Students should have the opportunity to restate their reasons for a particular position. Some individuals may want to add ideas to their reasoning after listening to comments during the discussion. Others may choose to change the position or significantly alter the reason which they presented initially. Several methods may promote this consideration:

1. Ask the students to write out their positions and their reasoning (as they did at the beginning of the class). Encourage them to add any new ideas or phrases which they heard during the discussion and which they thought were especially important.

2. Ask the students to record any changes which they discovered about their own thinking. Emphasize that some people may have experienced **no** change and that is very common. However, some people pick up ideas during a discussion. Give them an example of a change: "I still think that Sam should fill the food order when the truck arrives, but I also agree that the store owner does have a right to refuse credit to the striking mine workers! I had not thought of his feelings before."

NOTE: Another way to close a class discussion of a dilemma story is to ask the students if this dilemma seems real to them or if they have seen a similar situation in their lives. This technique also provides you with some degree of feedback concerning their interest in working with social and moral problems in the classroom.

The last segment of the transcript represents this final phase of the Teaching Process:

Teacher:
I notice that we only have about three minutes before the end of class. I would like you to do one last thing.

Think for a minute about all the different reasons which people gave for taking the **opposite** position from yours. For example, if you said at the beginning of the class that Sam should not fill the strikers' requests for groceries on credit, then think about the reasons which you have heard other people give for saying that Sam does have an obligation to help the strikers. On the back side of your 3 x 5 card, write down the most acceptable reason which you can remember for someone taking that other position.

Diana:
You mean that I have to pick some reason I agree with on the other side?

Teacher:
You may not agree with it, but pick the one most acceptable to you of all those you heard during the discussion.

Jerry:
I didn't have a position.

Teacher:
O.K., Jerry, would you now try to take a position? Which way are you leaning most and why? Write that on your card, if you will.

Joe:
Can I write down why I think some reason is most acceptable?

Teacher:
Certainly, I encourage it.

Debbi:
What if you have really changed your mind and now take the opposite position yourself? I'm even more undecided and maybe even feel that Sam should fill the order after all that talk about human rights.

Teacher:
O.K. Debbi, write that out on your card and indicate the kinds of things you heard which caused you to rethink your original position.

Students begin to write on the 3 x 5 cards and gather their books to leave.

Teacher:
One more thing! Tomorrow you will have a chance to ask some other people about their views on this problem. Mr. Waters, an officer of a local labor union, and Ms. Sheldon, who represents the city in all negotiations with the labor unions, have agreed to visit our class. You may even want to ask someone outside of class about his response to this story. See you tomorrow.

Students leave the room as the bell rings. As they hand the teacher their 3 x 5 cards, one student approaches to ask a question.

Jerry:
What do you think Sam should do, Mr. Peterson?

Teacher:
Well, it is a tough decision to choose between helping your friends and going against an employer or a rule of

some kind. I was attracted by one of the comments I heard during the discussion. Someone mentioned that the issue is larger than friends and food — that it is an issue of human rights, property, and the right of the store owner who also controls the mining company to control the food supply. Maybe Sam could help the strikers and still not help them break the law.

PAUSE

Teacher:
However, that position makes it seem like I'm merely looking for a way out of the dilemma. I guess right now that I think Sam should not fill the order; after all, by filling the order illegally, he could be helping to start some real violence. Maybe Sam should quit his job as manager if he thinks the store owner's position is unethical. I guess I can't turn my back on the fact that Sam doesn't actually have the right to give those groceries out on credit.

The last students leave the room trying to convince one another that Sam should be able to get out of this situation some way and still preserve his job and his friends.

The curriculum material, classroom atmosphere and Teaching Process discussed in the preceding sections provide one way to teach for moral reasoning. In review, the Teaching Process contains four major steps. In a classroom discussion, students need to: confront a specific social and moral dilemma; take an intial action position and develop reasons to support that position; test their reasons in small and large group discussions; and reflect on their initial position through some type of summarizing activity.

CHAPTER

SAMPLE MATERIALS AND SUGGESTIONS: INTERMEDIATE AND SECONDARY

USING MORAL DILEMMAS

To help you begin teaching for moral reasoning, we have provided a limited number of examples of curriculum materials. These hypothetical and real dilemma situations can be divided into three main categories: dilemmas related to a particular discipline such as history or English; dilemmas dealing with contemporary society; and dilemmas from the life-experience of elementary and secondary children. The dilemmas in this Handbook present examples from all of these categories. In some cases, the dilemmas have elements from more than one of the categories. *"Hey, Sam, The Truck Is Here,"* *The Ticket Scheme*, and *Elwood Hansen and the Cattle Protest* all have a definite historical context. These dilemma situations also have contemporary relevance. For example, *"Hey, Sam, The Truck Is Here"* could be placed in the context of the labor movement in the late 19th or early 20th century, or it could be integrated as part of a discussion about recent mining problems in the 1970's. *The Ticket Scheme* provides an example of a dilemma situation emerging from American literature as well as American history. The dilemma situation is taken from Richard Wright's book **Black Boy** which is set in the South during the 1920's. *Mrs. Bartholomew and Her Regular Customers*, *The Hospital Regulation*, and *Mercy Death* serve as examples of dilemmas developed out of contemporary issues in our society. *The Championship* relates to a contemporary issue as well as the immediate life-experience of the student.

The dilemma stories for the elementary grades involve situations predominantly from the life-experience category. These dilemmas include a variety of social or moral issues for younger students to consider. For example, *The Open Window* presents the issues of authority, friendship, and property. *The Surprise* also focuses on property, but it includes issues of truth, fairness, and obligation. Elementary level materials may also involve stories about contemporary society. Dilemmas may be found in various readings and in social studies lessons. The important key to teaching for moral reasoning involves the ability to use and develop dilemma stories from a life-experience situation, a contemporary event in society, or the existing curriculum material.

The dilemmas in this Handbook also provide you with a variety of media to help students confront moral dilemmas. In *Mercy Death*, the dilemma is presented by an actual newspaper article. In *The Ticket Scheme*, students confront the dilemmas as they read Richard Wright's novel **Black Boy**. The elementary stories include a film, a story which is told by the teacher, and a role-playing situation as methods of presentation. Teachers should try to use many different ways to present the stories.

Students should have opportunities to engage in a variety of activities as they move through the teaching process. For example, in *Mrs. Bartholomew and Her Regular Customers*, students engage in an alternative group strategy. In this grouping strategy, students role-take the various characters in the dilemma story and actually simulate the confrontation at the service station. This type of activity helps students experience a variety of learning environments. The story called *The Surprise* provides a similar experience for elementary students.

As teachers you have the greatest resources for the development of dilemma situations. Existing curriculum materials, films, filmstrips, current news events, and happenings in the local schools and communities represent excellent sources for creating dilemma situations. The dilemmas for elementary and secondary students included in this Handbook should serve only as a starting point.

Write your own dilemma situations following these guidelines. **First**, moral dilemmas should not be so complex that students have difficulty identifying the actual dilemma. The complexity of any dilemma should be related to the sophistication and ability level of students. This is true not only of the dilemma, but also the method by which the dilemma is introduced. **Second**, teachers should be sure to include the major elements necessary for a moral dilemma lesson. The dilemma situation must have a main character or group of characters that have to make a moral decision about what to do. The dilemma is posed by asking a "should" question. In any dilemma there should be a number of additional characters directly or indirectly affected by the decision of the main character. These additional characters provide students with the opportunity to consider the dilemma from different points of view. Each dilemma story also integrates one or more of the moral issues discussed previously in the Handbook. In any good dilemma situation, the central character should be pulled in a number of directions by the conflicting social norms presented in the dilemma. These conflicts create the genuine problem which serves as the focus for the discussion. A Teaching Plan accompanying each dilemma should contain appropriate alternative dilemmas or story expansions and a variety of probing questions.

Third, it is often easy to create dilemmas by working in small groups with other teachers. The process of developing moral dilemmas through small group work involves a number of steps. Initially, teachers working together should brainstorm ideas for moral situations that fall within the three main categories of dilemmas. Next, the group should incorporate the main elements discussed in the previous paragraph. After the dilemma and the lesson plan have been developed, they should be field-tested in one or two classroom situations. In the field-test situation, teachers should ask for student input as to whether the situation being discussed really constitutes a dilemma. Students serve as an invaluable resource for the development and the refinement of good dilemma situations. Using the field-test experience, teachers should then revise the dilemma and lesson plan for regular use in the course of study.

At some point you may want to give your students (elementary or secondary) an opportunity to create their version of a dilemma story. By doing this, you involve them in the identification of issues which are important to them and you also help them to understand more fully the process which you are sharing with them.

If you are interested in using this approach to help your students begin looking at social and moral issues, we suggest the following:

1. **Try it out!** Select the dilemma story which you think your students will enjoy discussing, and give it a try!

2. **Don't expect instant success.** Many teachers have indicated that these materials and this approach provided the basis for a "fantastic teaching experience." They often talk about how involved and serious students can become when discussing a social or moral problem. However, we know that leading an exciting discussion, asking the right question, keeping the focus on the moral issue, and getting students to talk to each other is a big job and takes practice. It works better and better with continued use.

3. **Refer to this Handbook often.** Use this as a guide and a workbook. Re-read Chapter 2, "The Dilemma Story," when you first try to write or develop your own. Review the transcript and check out the kinds of questions which seem to promote student discussion.

4. **Concentrate on the classroom climate.** You will set the scene for discussion. Classrooms can be informal and yet very serious and structured. They can be loud, yet remain focused on the discussion at hand. Students need to feel that you think the stories and issues are genuine and are a natural part of the course of study. They have a right to know why you think social and moral issues should be examined in

the classroom. Ask for their opinion on the dilemma stories, especially as to whether they seem real. The mining town where Sam lives may be a thousand miles from where they live, but the issues of friendship, obligation, and the law are part of their lives. They need to feel this as they discuss *"Hey, Sam, The Truck Is Here."*

5. **Think through some of the stories yourself.** What do you think is the right thing to do? Why? What other points of view should be considered? How does the story relate to the context of your course or the lives of your students? This will help you prepare to use the teaching plan and will also help you to begin thinking about social and moral issues, a task which we think is important.

CURRICULUM MATERIALS

DILEMMA ONE:

THE CHAMPIONSHIP

According to PA House Bill #225A, local school districts cannot receive state funds without providing equal opportunities for girls to participate in athletics. School districts must show that they are spending money to include girls on their athletic teams.

Prior to the track season Coach Dobisc of Larimer High School learned that all high school coaches should make every effort to allow girls to compete on the varsity teams. Coach Dobisc and Mr. Burns, Larimer's athletic director, agreed that they would comply with the new state law.

During the tryouts, Patty Connors did extremely well in the 440 yard dash. Patty worked very hard and her time for the event was excellent, but several of the boys could run the 440 faster. Patty was about equal to Tom Mitchell, but not as good as John Mardi, Harold Laser, and Paul Badger.

Coach Dobisc told Patty that she had made the team and would run in the mile relay. Usually Paul, Harold, John, and Tom ran the important relay race, but the team agreed that Patty and Tom would alternate for each track meet. Tom would run in every other meet for the season. During the season, the team of Paul, Harold, John, and Tom went undefeated, winning five relay races. When Patty ran, the team won two and lost two.

May 15 was the big day. Seven teams would compete for the county championship. Larimer had a chance to win the county championship for the third straight year. As the meet progressed, it appeared that the mile relay could determine the championship. Patty knew that it was her turn to run on the relay team, and she was doing some warm-up exercises in preparation for the race.

The day before the county championship, Paul, Harold, and John had talked about the possibility that the championship might hinge on the last relay. They knew that they could win the mile relay if the all-boy team ran. They decided that if the last relay was crucial to the outcome of the meet, they would ask Patty to voluntarily withdraw. With only two events to go, the boys looked at the score board. Larimer was one point out of first place and followed by a team one point behind them.

Harold, John, and Paul decided to go ahead with their plan. They approached Patty as she was doing her warm-up exercises. Harold asked Patty to fake a pulled muscle and tell the coach that she could not run in the relay. The boys explained to Patty that Larimer High could win another championship if Tom could run with the team. Patty had to agree that the chances for a win would be better with Tom in the relay. She didn't know what to do.

TEACHING PLAN:

THE CHAMPIONSHIP

Part I: The Original Dilemma

Distribute class handout, *The Championship*, which describes the situation as the team approaches the final event. Make sure that the students understand the terminology in the dilemma and can state the nature of the dilemma.

Determine by a show of hands or in some other way whether the class feels Patty should agree to withdraw from the race.

If the class divides with at least one-third of the students on each side of the issue, choose one of the small group strategies listed on pp. 85-90 of this Handbook and proceed with the discussion, skipping the alternative dilemmas.

Part II: Alternative Dilemmas

If the class agrees that Patty SHOULD withdraw from the race, one of the following alternative dilemmas can be used to provoke disagreement.

A. A group of college scouts are in the stands to watch Patty run. They are considering her for a track scholarship to college. Should that make a difference in the decision Patty makes?

B. A newspaper from a large city is at the track meet to

do a special feature on Patty and "Girls in Athletics."
Should that make a difference in Patty's decision?

If the class agrees that Patty SHOULD NOT withdraw
from the race, one of the following alternative
dilemmas can be used to provoke disagreement.

A. Coach Dobisc also asks Patty to voluntarily withdraw
   for the benefit of the team and the Championship.
   Should that make a difference in the decision Patty
   makes?

B. Patty is only a junior and the boys are all seniors.
   Patty will have one more year of eligibility. Should
   that make a difference in the decision Patty makes?

C. The boys decide to boycott the relay race if Patty will
   not withdraw. Should that make a difference in the
   decision Patty makes?

Part III: Probe Questions

1. Is winning the Championship more important than
   giving Patty an opportunity to run in the race? Why?

2. What is Patty's obligation to the team and winning
   the Championship?

3. Should the fact that the coach and the team agree to
   let Patty run in alternate races be more important
   than the immediate situation of the Championship?
   Why?

4. How important is the state law in this situation?

121

5. From the point of view of Coach Dobisc, what should Patty do?

6. What is the purpose of athletic programs in schools?

7. Should women be allowed to participate in sports on an equal basis with men?

8. Should Patty go along with the request of the other team members?

9. Is it ever right to fake an injury?

DILEMMA TWO:

THE TICKET SCHEME

Literature serves as an excellent source for dilemma situations. For example, in **Black Boy**, Richard Wright relates a series of events surrounding his early life and his attempt to escape Southern society in the 1920's. In **Black Boy**, Wright traces certain demeaning experiences in school and various jobs. Wright finally is employed as a ticket taker in a theater. The following excerpt from **Black Boy** provides an excellent introduction for a moral dilemma discussion.

One of the boys at the hotel whispered to me one night that the only local Negro movie house wanted a boy to take tickets at the door.

"You ain't never been in jail, is you?" he asked me.

"Not yet," I answered.

"Then you can get the job," he said. "I'd take it, but I done it six months and they know me."

"What's the catch?"

"The girl who sells tickets is using a system," he explained. "If you get the job, you can make some good gravy."

If I stole, I would have a chance to head northward quickly; if I remained barely honest...I merely prolonged my stay, increased my chances of being caught, exposed myself to the possibility of saying the wrong word or doing the wrong thing and paying a penalty that I dared not think of. The temptation to venture into crime was too strong, and I decided to work quickly, taking whatever was in sight.... I knew that others had tried it before me and had failed, but I was hoping to be lucky.

My chances for getting the job were good; I had no past record of stealing or violating the laws. When I presented myself to the Jewish proprietor of the movie house I was immediately accepted. The next day I reported for duty and began taking tickets. The boss man warned me:

"Now, look, I'll be honest with you if you'll be honest with me. I don't know who's honest around this joint and who isn't. But if you are honest, then the rest are bound to be. All tickets will pass through your hands. There can be no stealing unless you steal."

I gave him a pledge of my honesty, feeling absolutely no qualms about what I intended to do. He was white, and I could never do to him what he and his kind had done to me. Therefore, I reasoned, stealing was not a violation of my ethics but of his...

During the first afternoon the Negro girl in the ticket office watched me closely and I knew that she was sizing me up, trying to determine when it would be safe to break me into her graft. I waited, leaving it to her to make the first move.

I was supposed to drop each ticket that I took from a customer into a metal receptacle. Occasionally the boss would go to the ticket window and look at the serial number with the number on the last ticket I had dropped into the receptacle. The boss continued his watchfulness for a few days, then began to observe me from across the street; finally he absented himself for long intervals.

A tension as high as that I had known when the white men had driven me from the job at the optician's returned to live in me. But I had learned to master a great deal of tension now...

While I was eating supper in a nearby cafe one night, a strange Negro man walked in and sat beside me.

"Hello, Richard," he said.

"Hello," I said. "I don't think I know you."

"But I know you," he said smiling.

Was he one of the boss's spies?

"How do you know me?" I asked.

"I'm Tel's friend," he said, naming the girl who sold the tickets at the movie.

I looked at him searchingly. Was he telling me the truth? Or was he trying to trap me for the boss? I was already thinking and feeling like a criminal, distrusting everybody.

"We start tonight," he said.

"What?" I asked, still not admitting that I knew what he was talking about.

"Don't be scared. The boss trusts you. He's gone to see some friends. Somebody's watching him and if he starts back to the movie, they'll phone us," he said.

I could not eat my food...

"It'll work this way," he explained in a low, smooth tone. "A guy'll come to you and ask for a match. You give him five tickets that you'll hold out of the box, see? We'll give you the signal when to start holding out. The guy'll give the tickets to Tel; she'll resell them all at once, when a crowd is buying at the rush hour. You get it?"

I DID NOT ANSWER. I knew that if I were caught I

would go to the chain gang. But was not my life already a kind of chain gang? What, really, did I have to lose?

"Are you with us?" he asked.

I still did not answer. He rose and clapped me on the shoulder and left. I trembled as I went back to the theater. Anything might happen, but I was used to that...Had I not felt it when I walked home from the optical company that morning with my job gone?...Had I not felt it all a million times before? I took the tickets with sweaty fingers. I waited. I was gambling; freedom or the chain gang. There were times when I felt that I could not breathe. I looked up and down the street; the boss was not in sight. Was this a trap?

The man I had met in the cafe came through the door and put a ticket in my hand.

"There's a crowd at the box office," he whispered. "Save ten, not five. Start with this one."[1]

Should Richard join the ticket scheme to gain money to go North?

[1]Abridged from pp. 177-179 in **Black Boy** by Richard Wright Copyright, 1937, 1942, 1944, 1945 by Richard Wright. By permission of Harper & Row, Publishers, Inc.

TEACHING PLAN:

THE TICKET SCHEME

Part I: The Original Dilemma

Distribute the class handout, *The Ticket Scheme*, which describes the situation that Richard Wright faces. Make sure that the students understand the terminology in the dilemma and can state the circumstances and the nature of the dilemma.

Determine by a show of hands or in some other way how the class feels about whether Richard should join the scheme.

If the class divides with at least one-third of the students on each side of the issue, choose one of the small group strategies listed on pp. 85-90 of this Handbook, and proceed with the discussion, skipping the alternative dilemmas.

Part II: Alternative Dilemmas

If the class agrees that Richard SHOULD participate in the scheme, choose one of the following alternative dilemmas to provoke disagreement.

A. Suppose the owner of the theater has promised Richard a good raise if he works out well in the first month. Should that make a difference in the decision that Richard makes?

B. The owner of the theater has helped Wright's family

127

in the past. Should that make a difference in the decision that Richard makes?

If the class agrees that Richard SHOULD NOT participate in the scheme, choose one of the following alternatives to provoke disagreement.

A. The owner has a policy of charging Blacks more than he does the Whites for admission to the theater. Should this make a difference in Wright's decision?

B. Richard's family needs money to help with some medical bills for his mother who is seriously ill. Should this influence Richard's decision?

Part III: Probe Questions

1. What obligation does Richard have to the theater owner?

2. Should Richard consider that he has made a pledge to the theater owner?

3. From the point of view of his family, what should Richard do?

4. From the point of view of the customers, what should Richard do?

5. What is the importance of property rights?

6. Should the fact that Richard has experienced much

discrimination at the hands of Whites make any difference in his decision? Why?

7. Is it ever right to break a law?

DILEMMA THREE:

ELWOOD HANSEN
AND THE CATTLE PROTEST

Elwood Hansen's truck suddenly hit the edge of the road and the right front tire went into the snow-filled ditch. He would never make the meeting now. Elwood was furious! He had not been paying attention to the road; he had been thinking about what he would say at the meeting. Now he would have to walk to the nearest farm house and call Hank Stofer at the meeting hall.

As Elwood walked through the snow, he pulled a piece of paper out of his pocket and read it once more:

> *PROTEST PRICES*
> — HALF THE CATTLE RANCHERS IN DELAWARE COUNTY WILL GO BANKRUPT UNLESS WE PROTEST.
> — IF WE SHOW THAT WE WILL SHOOT OUR CATTLE RATHER THAN TAKE THEM TO MARKET, PEOPLE WILL LISTEN TO OUR SIDE OF THE STORY.
> — EVERYONE MUST JOIN IN THE PROTEST. IF ONE RANCHER TAKES HIS CATTLE TO MARKET, THE PROTEST WILL BE LOST.

Every cattle rancher in Delaware County was being hurt by the economy. The Cattlemen's Association had discussed a plan to protest the high price of feed material and the low market price they get for their cattle. Leaders of the Association suggested that farmers should start shooting their cattle rather than sell them for a low price. This was the only way they could force a better price for their cattle and stay in business.

Elwood had a small ranch, and he wasn't sure whether he and his family could make it if he didn't take his cattle to market. He also knew that the Association expected every rancher to cooperate in the protest. Elwood wondered what he should do. If he joined the protest, and it succeeded in raising market prices, the cattle ranches in Delaware County, (including Elwood's) might survive the economic crisis. If he took his cattle to market now, he and his family could at least make it through the winter and maybe sell the ranch in the Spring, although he really did not want to give up his ranch. Hank Stofer would be waiting for Elwood's answer.

Elwood walked to the farm house, asked to use the phone and dialed the number at the meeting hall where the ranchers were voting.

Should he tell Ed that he will go along with the protest?

TEACHING PLAN:

ELWOOD HANSEN AND THE CATTLE PROTEST

Part I: The Original Dilemma

Distribute class handout, *Elwood Hansen and the Cattle Protest*, which describes Elwood Hansen and the cattle ranchers. Make sure that the students understand the terminology in the dilemma and can state the nature of the dilemma which Elwood faces.

Determine by a show of hands or in some other way how the class feels about whether Elwood should go along with the protest.

If the class divides with at least one-third of the students on each side of the issue, choose one of the small group strategies listed on pp. 85-90 of this Handbook, and proceed with the discussion, skipping the alternative dilemmas.

Part II: Alternative Dilemmas

If the class agrees that Elwood Hansen SHOULD go along with the protest, one of the following alternative dilemmas can be used to provoke disagreement.

A. Elwood had planned on buying 300 acres of land which joined his property. He had saved his money and waited for the opportunity to add to his small ranch. However, if he participates in the protest, he will have to use his savings just to survive the winter. He will not be able to buy the iand. Should he still go along with the protest?

B. What if Elwood knew that the slaughtered cattle were going to be buried and that some needy families could use the food? Should he go along with the protest?

If the class agrees that Elwood Hansen SHOULD NOT go along with the protest, one of the following alternative dilemmas can be used to provoke disagreement.

A. The Cattlemen's Association had given Elwood a loan when he was in real trouble. Now his friends are counting on a unified vote. They helped Elwood, and they want him to go along with the protest. Should he?

B. The treasurer of the Cattlemen's Association called Elwood and told him that the Association would give him the money to get through the winter if he would join the protest. It is very important that **all** of the ranchers protest so that everyone knows that they are serious. Should Elwood agree to protest?

Part III: Probe Questions

1. Should ranchers protest if they think they are not getting the best price for their cattle? Why or why not?

2. Does Elwood have an obligation to go along with his friends and the Cattlemen's Association?

3. Should Elwood be more concerned about his family than about the welfare of all ranchers in Delaware County? Why or why not?

4. How might Elwood explain to Hank Stofer that he plans **not** to join or support the protest?

5. How might Elwood explain to a poor mother of seven hungry children why the cattlemen plan to shoot and bury cattle rather than take them to the meat packing plant?

DILEMMA FOUR:

THE HOSPITAL REGULATION

The security guard at the factory had just finished his lunch and was walking around the loading dock on Emerson Street. As he turned the corner to climb the stairs, he nearly tripped over the twisted body of a man. The man was moving around on the pavement of the parking lot and appeared to be in great pain. The guard turned the man slowly and found a very severe wound on the man's chest. The man was losing a lot of blood from the injury.

The guard knew that the man needed medical attention fast. The guard ran one block down Emerson Street to Community Hospital to seek help for the badly injured man. He raced into the emergency entrance and ran from room to room looking for help. At first he only found a mother with her hysterical child who had just fallen from a tree and broken an arm. As he went out of the treatment room, he met the nurse who was on duty in the emergency room. He quickly told her the story and urged her to follow him up the street to help the man. The nurse told him that the interns were all out on other calls and she could not leave the hospital. The guard insisted that the man would die without her help and told her to follow him to the parking lot. As the guard turned to rush out the door and return to the injured man, the nurse pointed to a large sign on the wall of the emergency room:

> HOSPITAL EMPLOYEES
> MAY NOT LEAVE THE BUILDING
> WHEN ON DUTY

The nurse turned and the guard was gone. She wanted to help, but she knew that the hospital rule was strictly enforced.

Should she follow the guard to help the injured man or stay at her duty station in the emergency room?

TEACHING PLAN:

THE HOSPITAL REGULATION

Part I: The Original Dilemma

Distribute class handout which describes the nurse

and the injured man. Make sure that the students understand the terminology in the dilemma and can state the nature of the dilemma which the nurse faces.

Determine by a show of hands or in some other way how the class feels about whether the nurse should follow the guard to help the injured man or stay at her duty station in the emergency room.

If the class divides with at least one-third of the students on each side of the issue, choose one of the strategies listed on pp. 85-90 of this Handbook, and proceed with the discussion, skipping the alternative dilemmas.

Part II: Alternative Dilemmas

If the class agrees that the nurse SHOULD follow the guard, one of the following alternative dilemmas can be used to provoke disagreement.

A. Two weeks prior to this incident another nurse and an intern on duty in the emergency room of Community Hospital left the hospital to render first aid at the scene of an automobile accident near the hospital. They were both fired from the hospital staff.

B. The mother of the hysterical child pleaded with the nurse not to leave. She insisted that the child might go into shock and she would not know what to do.

If the class agrees that the nurse SHOULD NOT follow the guard, but stay in the emergency room and obey the regulation, one of the following alternative dilemmas can be used to provoke disagreement.

A. What if the nurse knew that her brother worked at that factory?

B. What if the nurse knew from the description of the wound that the man would probably die without her medical assistance?

Part III: Probe Questions

1. Does the nurse have an obligation to try to save the man's life?

2. Does the nurse have an obligation to obey the hospital regulation?

3. Does the nurse have an obligation to the woman and the child in the emergency room?

4. From the point-of-view of the woman in the emergency room, what should the nurse do?

5. From the point-of-view of another worker at the factory, what should the nurse do?

6. Is it ever right to break a rule?

7. What if the nurse refuses to go to the man's aid and he dies? Should she be held responsible in any way?

8. If the nurse does go to the factory to help the man,

should she be punished by the hospital administration for breaking a rule?

DILEMMA FIVE:

MERCY DEATH

Situations involving moral issues surround us. Articles in newspapers, programs on television, and events in our community confront us with real-life moral dilemma stories. This newspaper story appeared in the **Pittsburgh Press** (see p. 138). Read the article carefully, and then return to this page.

Many people have discussed whether or not Mr. Waters should be punished for helping his wife commit suicide — or killing her (as some people insist).

— Some people say "Let him go free."

— Some say Mr. Waters should get at least a two-year prison sentence.

— Others say that Mr. Waters should get a ten-year prison sentence for taking a life.

Which statement do you agree with?

Man Charged In Wife's Mercy Death

PONTIAC, Mich. (UPI) — Robert Waters told his wife of 40 years he loved her, then kissed her goodby; Minutes later, she was dead.

Waters, a 65-year-old former high school principal, has been charged with manslaughter in the Nov. 13 death of his wife Kathleen. He pleaded innocent and was released on bond.

Police said Waters was responsible for his wife's death because he helped her get into a motor-running auto in the couple's garage, then closed the door.

Waters said his wife was despondent because of failing health and wanted to commit suicide. He said he could not talk her out of it.

"In the car he asked her if she was sure this was what she wanted," Oakland County Prosecutor L. Brooks Patterson said.

"She said yes," Patterson said. "And then she said to kiss her goodby and they expressed their love for one another. And then he got out of the car."

Mrs. Waters died of carbon monoxide poisoning.

Waters pleaded innocent to a charge that he "did willfully, feloniously, negligently and knowingly, but without malice or premeditation, kill and slay Kathleen Waters."

"This couple was very close," Patterson said. "But I am a servant of the law and am obliged to carry it out." [2]

[2]Reprinted by Permission of United Press International.

TEACHING PLAN:

MERCY DEATH

Part I: The Original Dilemma

Distribute class handout, *Mercy Death*, which describes Mr. Waters. Make sure that the students understand the terminology in the dilemma story. Determine how the class responds to the three statements about what should happen to Mr. Waters. If the class members disagree about the statements, you may select a particular small group strategy and ask the students to prepare a full class discussion of the action which should be taken in regard to Mr. Waters.

If the class agrees on what should happen to Mr. Waters, use one of the following alterations of the dilemma story.

Part II: Alternative Dilemmas

If the class agrees that they **SHOULD** let Mr. Waters go free, use the following alteration:

What if Mr. Patterson, the prosecutor, established that Mr. and Mrs. Waters had not been very close for several years and that their marital problems had something to do with Mrs. Waters' depression. Yes, she was in ill health, but that was not the only reason for her desire to commit suicide. Should Mr. Waters still go free?

If the class agrees that Mr. Waters SHOULD NOT go free, use the following alteration:

What if Mr. Waters' attorney could establish that Mrs. Waters was dying from a very painful and rare disease? The disease had no known cure, and Mrs. Waters wanted very much to die peacefully, without the trauma of many months in a hospital. Should Mr. Waters still be punished?

Part III: Probe Questions

1. Does a person have the right to decide when he will die?

2. Do you think Mr. Waters had an obligation to honor his wife's wish to commit suicide?

3. Should a person suffering from a terminal and painful illness be allowed to end his life when he chooses?

4. Should society try to prevent suicides? Why or why not?

5. Should an individual be punished for not preventing a suicide? Why or why not?

DILEMMA SIX:

MRS. BARTHOLOMEW AND HER REGULAR CUSTOMERS

Mrs. Bartholomew had owned and operated a local gas station for almost 20 years. She had built the small business slowly and often had trouble competing with the large company-owned stations in the area. She did manage to make enough money to raise her family and support her husband who was an invalid. Her small station thrived mostly because she had old-time, regular customers. The gasoline shortage threw everyone into a panic — everyone needed gasoline badly.

Mrs. Bartholomew felt that her regular customers had been loyal to her for years (even when her gas was two or three cents higher than other stations) and that they deserved her loyalty now. Mrs. Bartholomew also feared that she would lose the regular customers if she couldn't provide them with gasoline; so, she decided to sell gas only to her regular customers.

People began pulling into her station with their tanks almost empty and asking her to sell them gas. They were not regular customers so she refused to sell to them. One woman told Mrs. Bartholomew that the ''regular customer'' policy was against the law and that she intended to report her. Other customers argued that the policy was unfair and that she should treat everyone equally.

TEACHING PLAN:

MRS. BARTHOLOMEW AND HER REGULAR CUSTOMERS

Part I: The Original Dilemma

Distribute class handout which describes Mrs. Bartholomew and her regular customers. Make sure that the students understand the terminology in the dilemma and can state the nature of the dilemma which Mrs. Bartholomew faces.

Determine by a show of hands or in some other way how the class feels about whether Mrs. Bartholomew should sell gas to everyone or only to her regular customers.

If the class divides with at least one-third of the students on each side of the issue, choose one of the strategies listed on pp. 85-90 of this Handbook, and proceed with the discussion, skipping the alternative dilemmas.

Part II: Alternative Dilemmas

If the class agrees that Mrs. Bartholomew SHOULD sell gas only to her regular customers, one of the following alternative dilemmas can be used to provoke disagreement.

A. Mrs. Bartholomew was told that she could be sued for her "regular customer" policy.

B. The "regular customer" policy had caused a lot of trouble. Several fights had started. One of her attendants had been cut by glass when a brick went through her plate window; several tires had been stolen from her display case; and a child was almost hit by a car which went speeding out of her station when she told them about the policy.

If the class agrees that Mrs. Bartholomew SHOULD NOT sell gas only to her regular customers, one of the following alternative dilemmas can be used to provoke disagreement.

A. Many of Mrs. Bartholomew's regular customers had asked her specifically to save gasoline for them and had indicated that if she couldn't, they would take their business elsewhere.

B. Mrs. Bartholomew had signed an agreement with most of her regular customers promising to sell them all the gasoline they wanted.

Part III: Probe Questions

1. Is it fair for a business person to make special deals for certain people or old-time customers? Why or why not?

2. Is it right for Mrs. Bartholomew's regular customers to expect her to give them special treatment?

3. Should there be a law prohibiting gas stations from selling gas to their regular customers first? Why?

4. If the attendant knows that there is a law against selling to special customers, should he report Mrs. Bartholomew to the authorities? Why or why not? Should someone else report her?

5. From the point-of-view of a regular customer, is Mrs. Bartholomew's policy fair? Why?

A SMALL ROLE-PLAYING GROUP STRATEGY:

MRS. BARTHOLOMEW AND HER REGULAR CUSTOMERS

A strategy which works particularly well with this story involves a role-taking situation. If your class has divided somewhat evenly over the final question in the story (for example: 14 say that she should sell to everyone and 19 say that she should stick to her "regular customer" policy), break the class into four groups, two groups representing each position. Ask the groups to discuss the reasons for their position. While the small groups meet, move to each group and give the following tasks:

Group 1 (sell to everyone) — Tell this group to select 2 or 3 people who will take the role of customers seeking gas at Mrs. Bartholomew's station — they are not regular customers, however. The rest of the group should help these individuals prepare the reasons they will use to try to convince Mrs. Bartholomew to sell them gasoline.

Group 2 (sell to everyone) — Same task as above.

Group 3 (supporting the "regular customer" policy) — Ask this group to select 2 or 3 people who will take the role of regular customers who arrive at Mrs. Bartholomew's for gasoline. The entire group should help them prepare to discuss the policy with the others who also come for gas.

Group 4 (supporting the "regular customer" policy) — Ask this group to select 3 individuals to take the following roles:

Mrs. Bartholomew (or her oldest son)
A cousin of the family who works at the station
A young high school student who works at the station

The group should help these people prepare to defend their "regular customer" policy.

Begin the role-taking session by asking the participating customers to line up their chairs or desks as if they were in a line waiting to get to the pumps. Ask Mrs. Bartholomew and the attendants to stand (the rest of the class can sit on the periphery of the station setting). Suggest to the class that Mrs. Bartholomew and the cousin are busy pumping gas and that the other attendant is walking from car to car identifying the regular customers. Instruct the attendant to ask any others waiting in the line to pull out and go to some other station.

Sit down and watch the discussion as Mrs. Bartholomew and the service station crew try to convince people who are waiting for gasoline to leave the line.

Eventually draw the students on the outer circle into the discussion and focus on the issues involved in the dilemma story. [3]

[3]Some of the dilemma stories presented in this chapter were originally developed or adapted as part of the Responsible Citizenship Project, and ESEA Title III Project sponsored by the Pennsylvania Department of Education and the Allegheney Intermediate Unit, Pittsburgh, Pennsylvania 15212.

146

CHAPTER

SAMPLE MATERIALS AND SUGGESTIONS: ELEMENTARY

SIX STEPS IN THE CLASSROOM PROCESS

Using the Teaching Process in the elementary classroom can be especially exciting. Although the dilemma stories should deal with less abstract issues, younger students have repeatedly demonstrated a willingness to engage in class discussions of moral dilemma stories. **You may find it helpful at this point to read the section "Using Moral Dilemmas" on pp. 112-117 in Chapter Five.**

The Teaching Process described in this Handbook was designed specifically with intermediate and secondary school classrooms in mind. However, the four steps of the Teaching Process still apply in discussions at the elementary level. Elementary teachers should review the following steps when using the process with younger students.

1. Warm-up Exercises

Elementary students need an opportunity to begin thinking about the general circumstances or context of the dilemma situation. For example, when introducing the dilemma story, *The Surprise*, (found on page 157 in this Handbook) involving a brother and sister who go to buy some materials at a hobby store, a warm-up exercise might involve asking the following questions:

a. How many of you have ever been in a hobby store?

b. What kinds of things do you find in a hobby store? (Make a list).

c. Have you ever been in a store that was so crowded that there were two clerks working at the counter, one collecting money with the other putting the purchases in a bag for the customer?

d. Have you noticed how fast some clerks put things into the bags after you pay for them?

These questions elicit responses which allow students to begin identifying early with the circumstances of the dilemma and create a more genuine context for the dilemma story which follows. Pictures, a short film segment, or a newspaper story could also serve as appropriate warm-up exercises to establish the context for a dilemma story.

2. **Presentation**

We have suggested that dilemma stories may be presented in a variety of ways. Many of the dilemmas for intermediate and secondary school classrooms involve a written format. Obviously dilemma stories for elementary students should not be repeatedly presented in this format. A variety of films, filmstrips, and audio-tapes are available to be used with younger students. Teachers may act as storytellers and relate dilemma stories to students as a method of presenting the situation. You may also set up role-playing or role-taking situations in which students act out characters in a dilemma story and discuss the right thing to do from that character's point of view. This process also helps students begin to develop skills of empathizing and understanding issues from another point of view. Picture cards, drawings on the chalkboard, and a puppet show are creative ways of involving younger students in dilemma stories.

3. **Asking Initiating Questions**

It is not as helpful or productive to ask younger children to immediately indicate tentative positions on the dilemma by raising their hands or writing down answers as is suggested for the older grades. Elementary students need a chance to begin discussing the story and trying to understand the different characters involved. The following steps should follow the presentation of the dilemma story:

a. Carefully clarify the circumstances, the identity of the various characters, and any difficult terms or unusual situations. Let the students clarify as much as possible.

b. Ask the students to identify the problem for the central character(s) in the story.

c. Ask several general probing questions, and try to give several students a chance to indicate their positions. This initial questioning process will do two things:

1) give the students a chance to make their views
known (stating an individual position), and

2) give the leader an indication whether the
dilemma story has produced disagreement
among class members (determine a class
position).

d. At this point the teacher can decide to:

1) continue with a discussion involving the entire
class, using probe questions and making sure
that students talk to each other about their
positions, or

2) use a small group strategy to continue the
discussion, or

3) introduce a story expansion for the dilemma
story which will allow students to consider
another aspect of the dilemma.

*NOTE: All of these procedures should involve
students in an examination of reasoning related
to the moral issues in the story.*

For example, after a teacher has introduced the
story, *The Surprise*, and told the class about Lenny
and Sarah's trip to the hobby store, the teacher
would then set up a role-taking situation in which
two students could read through the script of Lenny
and Sarah. Two students could do this in the middle
of a circle with the rest of the class observing. After

the students have read through the script, the teacher would begin to determine how the class agrees or disagrees in their recommendation for action involving Lenny and Sarah. The teacher can also determine at this time the various positions which individual students have taken on the dilemma question. To do this, a teacher may ask a question like, ''What do you think Lenny and Sarah should do at this time?'' As students begin to respond with recommendations for Lenny and Sarah, a teacher can judge whether the class is in agreement over the action position or whether there is some conflict concerning Lenny and Sarah's dilemma. From this initial phase, a teacher can immediately begin to probe for reasoning as to why students think the way they do.

4. **Group Work**

Elementary students can work best in small groups if the task is clear and if they are genuinely involved in a discussion of the dilemma story. Therefore, small group work with elementary children often comes later in a class discussion of a moral dilemma. In the secondary classrooms, small group work is often used as a way of warming up students for a full class discussion. In an elementary classroom, students need a chance to examine the characters in the dilemma and to hear other students' views prior to focusing on a specific task in a small group. Small group work can then involve role-taking sessions or specific tasks which allow students to continue thinking about the dilemma story. For example, after students have discussed a dilemma story for a short time, a teacher may ask them to work in groups of three and to produce a drawing or picture which shows the way the story should end. Teachers can create small groups in such a way that students with slightly different points of view will be able to work together to produce an ending to a dilemma story. In this way, a discussion of the characters and the issues in the dilemma will continue while students work cooperatively on a task involving art. Many times, however, an elementary class can continue the discussion without breaking into small groups. If the class is relatively small, the teacher can keep the group together and use the probe questions and story expansions to continue the discussion.

5. **Story Expansions**

When a teacher discovers that the initial dilemma story does not create a conflict for the students or when the students seem to finish a discussion of the initial dilemma story, another aspect may be presented. Rather than presenting a series of alterations to the dilemma as indicated in the teaching plan presented for the secondary classrooms, we suggest that the elementary dilemma stories have a series of story expansions. A story expansion may be thought of as an additional chapter of the dilemma story. For example, if the students have discussed Lenny and Sarah's situation to the point where it no longer seems productive or if the students all agree that Lenny and Sarah should not return their surprises to the hobby store, the following story expansion might be presented to the class:

Lenny and Sarah agreed that they would not return the extra things they had received from the hobby store. Two days later in school, Lenny met his good friend Dave on the playground. After they had finished a hard game of kickball, David and Lenny sat down on the grass and began talking about their weekend. David started telling Lenny about what had happened to him on Saturday. He had spent his allowance to get a new race car at the hobby store and when he got home he did not have his race car in his sack, but instead had somebody else's plastic airplane. David was very upset because he had saved his money to buy this new race car and the hobby store clerk goofed him up. David even told Lenny that he had gone back to the hobby store but he could not prove that he did not get his race car. The hobby store manager told him that things had been mixed up and that maybe whoever got his race car by mistake would return it.

This story expansion continues the story of Lenny and Sarah and presents Lenny specifically with a new dilemma very tightly focused on obligation, friendship, and fairness. Here is another example of the class discussion revolved around the idea that Lenny might decide to take his material back and Sarah might decide not to take hers. Students may initially discuss whether Lenny has an obligation to make Sarah take her things back or to tell their parents about Sarah's decision to keep the extra material. Some of the students will probably say that Lenny should take his material back and that he should not feel responsible for Sarah's decision. The following story expansion could be used as a way of continuing the discussion and helping students examine their reasoning involving this decision:

> On Monday afternoon, Lenny returns to the hobby store and gives the store manager the racing car and extra tube of glue which he had received on Saturday. The store manager thanked Lenny very much and told him how mixed up things had been on Saturday and how disappointed some of the other children had been because things were so confused. The store manager told Lenny about one little girl who got home with a package of clay when she had purchased some beautiful beads and how the girl had returned to the store to ask the store manager if anyone had brought her beads back. The store manager asked Lenny if he knew anything about anyone who had received some extra packages of beads in their sack.

The story expansions which are built into the teaching plans for elementary dilemma stories provide students with opportunities to examine a number of dilemma issues and to continually re-examine their reasoning involving the right thing to do.

6. Closing Strategies for Reflection

Elementary students need specific suggestions for continuing to think about the issues involved in a dilemma story. For example, near the end of a class discussion, a teacher may suggest to students that they think to themselves about what they would do if they found a surprise in their sack when they

155

returned from making purchases at a hobby store or grocery store or in some other situation. These closing suggestions are not meant to provoke continued discussion of the dilemma but, instead, to suggest to students that they keep thinking about the situation. Another example of a closing strategy would be to suggest to students that they share the dilemma story with their parents and get their parents involved in a discussion. A teacher could also pose a question which summarizes the issue discussed during the class session. For example, for the dilemma story *"Who Needs Rules?"* on page 172, involving the brother and sister who want to keep a dog in the apartment building which expressly forbids animals, a teacher may ask students to silently consider the question, ''Why do we need rules?'' A teacher may even ask the class to consider a universal kind of question: ''Why is your solution to this problem the very best of all?'' Closing strategies are a specific part of the dilemma process. They are designed to suggest to students that they continue thinking about the issues which have been discussed as part of the dilemma story. Elementary students will often act on the suggestions and take the dilemma story home, share it with their parents, and involve the family in discussing social and moral issues.

CURRICULUM MATERIALS

DILEMMA ONE:

THE SURPRISE

Lenny and his sister Sarah went to the hobby store on Saturday morning to buy some supplies. The store was very crowded, and lots of other boys and girls were lined up at the counter paying for model airplanes, glue, beads, and other toys and materials. Lenny picked out several boxes of track for his race track which he had in the basement. He also found some glue and some pieces of wood which he would use to build houses and garages around the race track. Sarah found a package of beads and some brightly colored yarn which she planned to use to make a hanging basket for one of her mother's flower pots. Lenny and Sarah went to the counter to buy their supplies and had to stand in a crowd of other people also trying to buy things from the store. There were several clerks working to help the many people in the store. One clerk was taking money, and another clerk was putting the materials in sacks for the customers. Lenny and Sarah paid the clerk, picked up their sacks, and started home.

When they got to their house and looked in the sacks, they were surprised. In Lenny's sack he found a box with a new racing car in it and an extra tube of glue. In Sarah's sack she found a small paint set and two extra packages of beads which she had not picked out. Lenny and Sarah talked about what had happened:

Lenny:
Sarah, I found some extra things in my sack.

Sarah:
So did I. I wonder what happened.

Lenny:
I don't know. Maybe with all of those people trying to buy supplies at the hobby store, the man mixed up the orders.

Sarah:
Oh well, that's not our fault. Now I have some extra beads.

Lenny:
Yeah, and I got a race car which will really be great on my new track.

Sarah:
But you can't keep that race car. You didn't pay for it. It must belong to someone else.

Lenny:
Maybe it doesn't belong to me, but I've got it home now. Do you think I want to walk all the way back to the hobby store to give the race car back? What about your beads?

Sarah:
Yeah, I know. I'd like to keep the beads, but what if the store owner finds out that we have these things which we didn't pay for?

Lenny:
It's the store owner's fault. Besides, how's he going to find out?

Sarah:
But Mom or Dad might find out.

Lenny:
Yeah, that's right. But we don't have to tell them.

Sarah:
Oh, I don't know. Somebody else is going to miss these beads when they get home and look in their sack.

Lenny:
Yeah, and somebody probably spent their allowance to buy this race car and it ended up in my bag. But it sure would look neat on my track.

Sarah:
Maybe we should wait and the store will call and ask if we got some extra things.

Lenny:
Good idea. I'm going to go down and try out the race car.

Sarah:
Do you really think you should? Should I open the bag of beads?

TEACHING PLAN:

THE SURPRISE

A. Warm-Up Questions:

1. How many of you have ever been in a hobby store?

2. What kinds of things do you find in a hobby store? (Make a list).

3. Have you ever been in a store that was so crowded that there were two clerks working at the counter, one collecting money while the other put the purchases in a bag for the customer?

4. Have you noticed how fast some clerks put things into the bags after you pay for them?

B. Presentation:

Read or tell the story about Lenny and Sarah and their trip to the hobby store. Ask for two students to role-take the characters Lenny and Sarah and read through the script which provides the conversation between Lenny and his sister.

NOTE: Give these students an opportunity to read through the script prior to acting out their parts.

Let the actors sit in the center of a circle, facing each other as they hold the Lenny and Sarah conversation.

C. Initiating Questions:

Clarify the circumstances, terms, and characters in the story. The following questions should help to determine how individual students respond to the dilemma story and whether the class disagrees over the action position for the central characters in the story.

1. What do you think Lenny and Sarah should do?

2. Should Lenny take the car back to the hobby store right away?

3. Is it okay for Sarah to open the bag of beads?

4. Should Lenny and Sarah tell anyone else about their surprise? Whom should they tell?

5. What should Lenny and Sarah think about before they use the surprises they found in their bags?

NOTE: Be sure to give as many students as possible a chance to respond to the initiating questions so that you can determine if they have different viewpoints on the story. Frequently ask students to respond to another student comment. For example: "David, do you also agree with Lisa's comment, or do you have some other idea to add?" or "Susan, a lot of people here think it is okay for Lenny to keep the car. What do you think?"

You can decide to continue the discussion, use one of the small group strategies, or introduce a story expansion.

D. **Small Group Strategies:**

1. *Role-Taking:* Set up groups of three or four (or a matching number for the number of characters in the story) and give each student a role to take. For example, Lenny, Sarah, the store owner, Lenny's mother, a friend of Sarah or Lenny. Give the groups the following instructions:

   a. Your group of characters should talk about the best thing for Lenny and Sarah to do in this situation and why it is the best thing.

   b. Remember, use your own ideas about what you believe is right, but discuss these ideas as your character would talk about them. For example, if you are playing the store owner and you think Lenny should keep the car, then talk about how the store owner might agree that Lenny should keep it.

2. *Illustrating the ending:* Set up groups of three and give each group a large piece of drawing paper and crayons. Ask the group to talk about how the story should end and then make a drawing which illustrates that ending. Each group can then explain their drawing to the class and the teacher can ask probe questions which may promote additional discussion. The other students should also be encouraged to ask questions of the group which is presenting its drawing.

3. *Listing reasons:* Set up groups of three or four and give them the following tasks:

a. List two or three things which you think Lenny and Sarah should do because of their problem. Why are these things good to do?

b. List two or three things which you think they should **not** do. Why should Lenny and Sarah not do these things?

NOTE: A group strategy should always be followed up with a discussion which focuses on what happened in the small groups. At this point, the teacher can emphasize and provide questions concerning the reasoning for positions taken during the small group exercises.

E. **Story Expansion:**

If the initial dilemma story does not create a conflict for the students or when the students seem to finish a discussion of the initial story, another aspect may be presented. A story expansion may be thought of as an additional chapter of the dilemma story.

1. Lenny and Sarah decided to keep the surprises which were in their bags from the hobby store. That evening, Sarah's mother asked her how she was able to get so many different kinds of beautiful beads. How should she explain?

2. Lenny did use the race car on his track that afternoon. He raced his cars for almost two hours and the tires on the new car were almost worn out.

Lenny told Sarah about using the car which really wasn't his and asked her to promise that she wouldn't tell anyone. Sarah agreed. That evening Sarah and her father were working in the basement on a new playhouse which they were building. Sarah's father noticed the new car near Lenny's track and said: "I've never seen this car before. I wonder when Lenny bought this one. Sarah, do you know how Lenny got this new race car?"

F. Probe Questions

1. Is it fair for Lenny and Sarah to keep the surprises? Why or why not?

2. If the owner of the hobby store is a friend of their father, should Lenny and Sarah return the surprises? Why or why not?

3. Should Lenny and Sarah tell their parents about the surprises?

4. Should Lenny try out the race car even if he plans to take it back to the store?

5. If Lenny and Sarah disagree about whether to return the surprises, how should they solve their disagreement?

6. If Lenny and Sarah do not return the surprises and their parents find out, should they be punished in any way?

DILEMMA TWO:

THE OPEN WINDOW

Each evening right after dinner time, the big playground next to the school was always filled with kids. Kids from the neighborhood were always starting softball, kickball, or sometimes even volleyball games which lasted until it was almost dark. On this particular evening, Cindy, Jason, and Paul, along with a lot of other kids, had been playing kickball. It was almost dark and the game was about to break up when one of the girls shouted, "Hey, look what I found!" Eight or nine of the kids ran over to the side of the building to find out why the girl was shouting. One of the windows in the school was open. Jason had an idea: "Hey, let's boost each other up and go inside the school. That will be fun! No one will be in the school building except us, and we can have fun." The kids all agreed and one by one were boosted up through the window and into the classroom. Cindy was one of the last ones to come in through the window and the other kids had already gone out of the classroom and started running down the halls of the empty school. Cindy was afraid. She wasn't sure she wanted to be part of this. She knew she wasn't supposed to be inside the school after it was closed. She thought for a minute and decided that she better go home. It was almost dark, anyway. She crawled back out of the window, stretched as far as she could, jumped a short distance to the ground, and ran home.

The next day when Cindy arrived at school, she noticed that there was a lot of confusion. The teachers were talking out in the hall, and a lot of kids were talking and laughing in the classroom. Cindy soon found out what all the confusion was about. The principal visited each classroom and told the students what had happened the night before. Somebody had broken into the school the evening before and had been running around in the empty building. Whoever it was had turned all the chairs around so that they were backwards in several of the classrooms. They had taken the blanket from the nurse's office and had been sliding up and down the floors in the hall. They wrote a lot of silly things all over the chalkboards in several of the rooms, and they took the second graders' art display down off the wall near the gymnasium. The principal explained that this was more than just a prank. Students were not supposed to be in the school building after the school was closed. The teacher explained, "We are all proud of our school and we all have to take responsiblity for protecting the school and the building. If anyone in the class knows about what happened in the school building last night or who was involved, he should go to the principal some time during the day and tell the principal what he knows."

Should Cindy talk to the teacher or to the principal and explain what had happened the night before?

NOTE: It may not be uncommon for all of your students to agree that Cindy should keep quiet. The story expansion will be especially helpful for this story.

TEACHING PLAN:
THE OPEN WINDOW

A. **Warm-Up Questions:**

1. How many of you have ever played kickball or softball or some kind of game on the school playground after the school was closed?

2. Have you ever looked in the window of the school after it was closed?

3. Have you ever been playing with a group of your friends when someone said, ''Let's go do something.'' You were not sure whether you really wanted to do it or not, but you wanted to go along with your friends.

B. **Presentation:**

Tell the story about Cindy and her friends and the open window.

C. **Initiating Questions:**

Clarify the circumstances, terms, and characters in the story. The following questions should help to determine how individual students respond to the dilemma story and whether the class disagrees over the action position for the central character in the story.

1. Do you think Cindy should be upset by what the principal and the teacher have said?

2. Do you think she should talk to the principal or the teacher some time during the day?

3. Should she talk to her parents about what happened at the school?

4. If she tells the principal or the teacher about what happened the night before, should she mention that she was inside the school for a few minutes?

NOTE: Be sure to give as many students as possible a chance to respond to the initiating questions so that you can determine if they have different viewpoints on the story. Frequently ask students to respond to another student comment. For example, "David, do you also agree with Lisa's comment or do you have some other idea to add?" or "Susan, a lot of people here think that it's okay for Cindy to talk to the teacher about what happened. What do you think?"

You can decide to continue the discussion, use one of the small group strategies, or introduce a story expansion at this point. With this particular dilemma, the story expansions are especially helpful.

D. Small Group Strategies

1. *Role-Taking:* Set up groups of three or four or a matching number for the number of characters in the story, and give each student a role to take. For example, teacher, one of Cindy's parents, Cindy,

Jason, Paul, and a friend. Give the group the following instructions:

a. Your group of characters should talk about the best thing for Cindy to do in this situation and why it is the best thing.

b. Remember, use your own ideas about what you believe is right, but discuss these ideas as your character would talk about them. For example, if you were playing Cindy's mother and you think Cindy should not talk to the teacher, then you should talk about how Cindy's mother might agree that Cindy should keep quiet.

2. *Illustrating the Ending:* Set up groups of three and give each group a large piece of drawing paper and crayons. Ask the group to talk about how the story should end, then make a drawing which indicates that ending. Each group can explain the illustration to the class, and the teacher can ask probe questions which may promote additional discussion. The other students should also be encouraged to ask questions of the group which is presenting its drawing.

3. *Listing Reasons:* Set up groups of three or four and give them the following tasks:

List two or three things which you think Cindy should do because of this problem. Why are these things good to do?

List two or three things which you think Cindy

should **not** do. Why should Cindy not do these?

A group strategy should always be followed up with a discussion which focuses on what happened in the small groups.

At this point the teacher can emphasize and provide questions concerning the reasoning for positions taken during the small group exercise.

E. **Story Expansions:**

If the initial dilemma story does not create a conflict for the students or when the students seem to finish a discussion of the initial story, another aspect may be presented. A story expansion may be thought of as an additional chapter of the dilemma story.

1. Cindy decided not to say anything to the principal or the teacher. The rest of the school day she worried a lot about whether the kids would get into trouble and whether anybody would find out who was in the school building the night before. Just before she left to go home, she received a note to come to the principal's office. When she arrived in the principal's office, the principal told her that they knew about the night before. Mrs. Wilson, who lives right next door to the school, had called the principal and reported that she had seen Cindy jump from the window and run home. The principal asked Cindy why she had done all of the things in the school building.

2. During third period, Cindy learned about a

terrible accident which had happened in Room 107. The third grade classroom, 107, had a large aquarium with many beautiful fish. Everyone in the school enjoyed stopping by Room 107 some time during the year and looking at the fish. The students in 107 took good care of the aquarium and were very proud of all the different kinds of fish which they had. Whoever was in the school building the night before had knocked over the aquarium, had broken the glass, and all the fish had died. The class in Room 107 was very upset and angry about the people in the building who had done this. Cindy's brother, Bobby, was a third grader in Room 107. He talked to Cindy after school and told her that he knew she was playing at the school playground that night and that she must have some idea who went into the school. He wanted Cindy to tell him who the people were. Bobby promised not to go to the teacher or the principal, but he wanted Cindy to tell him who the people were who broke the aquarium in Room 107.

F. **Probe Questions:**

1. Is it right to go into a school building if you find a window open? Why or why not?

2. Should her friends be angry with Cindy if she tells the principal what happened?

3. Should Cindy say anything to any of the other students about who was involved in the open-window incident the night before?

4. Should Cindy say anything to her parents about what happened at school?

5. What was the worst thing that the students did in the school, write silly things on the chalkboard, turn all the desks around, take down the second graders' art display, or break the aquarium in Room 107?

6. If Cindy's friends are discovered and taken to the principal's office, should they be punished in any way for what they did?

DILEMMA THREE:

"WHO NEEDS RULES?"

Short segments of film provide an exciting medium for presenting dilemma stories to younger students. Encyclopaedia Britannica Educational Corporation has produced several films suitable for this teaching approach. The following excerpt from the Encyclopaedia Britannica Educational Corporation guide summarizes the first episode in the film. We have provided a specific teaching plan which can be used with the film.

"The film presents two situations in which children are torn between obeying or breaking a rule. In the first episode, Steve and Connie find a stray puppy in the park. Steve wants to keep it, but Connie reminds him of their apartment building's

172

rule prohibiting pets. Steve is concerned about the puppy's health, however, and decides to take the dog home to feed it. Connie also feels attached to the unfortunate pup, but reminds Steve of the rule and worries that the family will be evicted if a pet is discovered. Steve's desire to give the puppy a good home conflicts with Connie's practical observations. They are left to make their difficult decision as the projector is stopped. The viewers then consider what they would do in this situation.'' [1]

TEACHING PLAN:

"WHO NEEDS RULES?"

A. **Warm-Up Questions:**

1. How many of you have ever had a puppy?

2. How many of you have ever found a puppy in a park, on a playground or in your neighborhood?

3. Does anybody here live in an apartment building? Do you know whether apartment buildings have rules concerning animals or pets? What are some of the rules?

4. Have you ever heard of an apartment building that has a rule saying you cannot have pets in the building?

[1] From: **"Who Needs Rules?"** Encyclopaedia Britannica Educational Corporation. (Chicago, 1972.)

5. Who knows what an animal shelter is? What happens when puppies are taken to an animal shelter?

B. **Presentation:**

Show the first segment of the film to the class. Begin the film at the place where it shows a sign in the park and Connie and Steve playing with a Frisbee, searching for the Frisbee in the shrubbery, and finding a puppy. Run the film through the place where Steve says, "Look, I can't take care of him all by myself. But if you help, we can do it, at least for the summer. Come on, Connie, do we try it or not?" At this point, a narrator asks several questions. These questions can be used as part of the initiating questions for the discussion.

C. **Initiating Questions:**

Clarify the circumstances, terms, and characters in the story. The following questions should help to determine how individual students respond to the dilemma story and whether the class disagrees over the action position for the central characters in the story.

1. What should Steve and Connie do?

2. Why does the apartment have a rule against pets?

3. Do Steve and Connie have a right to break that rule?

4. Should Steve and Connie tell anyone else about their puppy in the storeroom?

174

5. What is the best thing for Steve and Connie to do so that they can help the puppy?

NOTE: Be sure to give as many students as possible a chance to respond to the initiating questions so that you can determine if they have different viewpoints on the story. Frequently ask students to respond to another student comment. For example: "David, do you also agree with Lisa's comment, or do you have some other idea to add?" or "Susan, a lot of people here think it's okay for Steve and Connie to keep the puppy. What do you think?"

You can decide to continue the discussion, use one of the small group strategies, or introduce a story expansion.

D. **Small Group Strategies:**

1. *Role-Taking:* Set up groups of three or four (or a matching number for the number of characters in the story) and give each student a role to take. For example, Steve, Connie, the apartment manager, and Steve and Connie's mother and father. Give the groups the following instructions:

    a. Your group of characters should talk about the best thing for Steve and Connie to do in this situation and why it is the best thing.

    b. Remember, use your own ideas about what you believe is right, but discuss these ideas as your character would talk about them. For example,

175

if you think Steve and Connie should keep the puppy, then talk about how the apartment owner might agree that Steve and Connie should keep it.

2. *Illustrating the Ending:* Set up groups of three and give each group a large piece of drawing paper and crayons. Ask the group to talk about how the story should end and then make a drawing which illustrates that ending. Each group can then explain their drawing to the class, and the teacher can ask probe questions which may promote additional discussion. The other students should also be encouraged to ask questions of the group which is presenting its drawing.

3. *Listing Reasons:* Set up groups of three or four and give them the following task:

List two or three things which you think Steve and Connie should do because of their problem. Why are these things good to do?

List two or three things which you think they should **not** do. Why should Steve and Connie not do these?

NOTE: A group strategy should always be followed up with a discussion which focuses on what happened in the small groups. At this point, the teacher can emphasize and provide questions concerning the reasoning for positions taken during the small group exercises.

E. Story Expansion:

If the initial dilemma story does not create a conflict for the students or when the students seem to finish a discussion of the initial story, another aspect may be presented. A story expansion may be thought of as an additional chapter of the dilemma story.

1. Steve and Connie decide to keep the puppy in the storeroom for a while. They take good care of the puppy, they bring it food and water, and stay for several hours each day. One evening, the apartment building manager knocks on the door of their apartment and begins talking with Steve and Connie's father. He tells them that several people have reported to him that Steve and Connie are keeping a puppy some place in the building. He wants to know if this is true and reminds Steve and Connie's father that he has signed an agreement not to have any pets in the building. If he breaks that agreement, the family will have to leave the apartment building within 30 days. The father comes into Connie's room and asks her if she and Steve have a puppy hidden in the building. The apartment building manager is standing behind the father. Connie doesn't know what to do. Her father says, "Come on Connie, either you do or you don't. Please tell me right now."

2. The next weekend, Steve and Connie went with their father to another city to visit their grandparents. They asked Jimmy, a friend of theirs who lives in the same building, to take care of the

puppy. Connie told Jimmy that he was responsible for the puppy. Steve showed Jimmy how to feed and water the puppy. They both told Jimmy how important it was that the puppy should not be turned loose on the street because it might be hurt. Steve and Connie left on their weekend trip. Jimmy took good care of the new puppy Friday night and all day Saturday. Sunday morning, Jimmy was sneaking into the storeroom to play with the puppy for a little while and to bring it fresh water. As he closed the door very quietly, the manager came down the hall and saw Jimmy in the storeroom. He walked into the storeroom, saw the puppy, and immediately began shouting at Jimmy. The manager told Jimmy that there was a rule against having pets in this building and that anybody who had a pet any place in the building could not continue to live there. The building manager told Jimmy that if he did not get rid of the puppy in an hour, his parents would be told. Jimmy told the manager he didn't know what to do with the puppy. The manager said that he would be back to check on Jimmy in an hour. He slammed the storeroom door and walked down the hall. Jimmy looked down at the puppy, not knowing what to do.

F. Probe Questions

1. Is it fair for Steve and Connie to bring the puppy into the apartment building?

2. Should Steve or Connie tell their father about the puppy they found and are keeping in the storeroom?

3. If Steve or Connie are asked by the manager if they have a dog hidden in the building, what should they say?

4. The puppy is in the storeroom for a long time, makes such a mess of the things, sometimes barking in the night, that the manager finds out and tells their father. Should Steve and Connie then be punished for breaking the rule?

5. Steve and Connie keep the puppy in the storeroom and tell the manager that they do not have a puppy hidden in the apartment building. Which is worse, breaking the rule or not telling the truth to the building manager?

7
CHAPTER

FREQUENTLY
ASKED
QUESTIONS

1. If Kohlberg's theory is correct in claiming that every person develops "naturally" through a universal sequence of stages, why should the classroom be involved in moral education at all?

Although the process is developmental, not everyone reaches his full capacity for moral maturity. Certainly there is little advantage in accelerating the sequence if everyone ends up at the same stage anyway. However, not everyone ends up at the same stage. In fact, only a small percentage of adults reach the postconventional morality, and it is possible to find adults as low as Stage 2. Therefore, the objective of the school is not to accelerate development, but to make sure that every person will eventually reach a mature level of moral reasoning.

2. How do you introduce the idea of moral dilemma discussions to students?

Prior to the discussion of the first moral dilemma story, you should spend some time talking with your students about values, decision making, reasoning, and a new teaching process which you as a teacher will be using. At this point, you may want to ask the students to define the word **dilemma** and possibly to give some examples of dilemmas which they face in their daily lives. The students might observe that a dilemma situation involves a set of circumstances that can present choices which do not always have clear cut right or wrong answers. Discussing a dilemma would involve trying to determine the rightness or wrongness of certain courses of action and to discuss the reasoning for recommending a particular decision. Next, the teacher may review the main steps in the teaching process. You may explain that the class period will be divided into a number of segments. During the class the students will be confronting a dilemma, taking a series of positions on what they think a particular character should do, working in small groups to complete specific tasks or answer questions, and exchanging viewpoints with other members of the class. You may even review with the students some of the objectives that you as a teacher have for these new lessons that deal with social and moral issues.

Given a moral dilemma in writing, orally, or in some other form, the students can:

1. State the facts and conditions of the dilemma in their own words.

2. State the moral dilemma implicit in the situation.

3. State a position on the dilemma.

4. State one or more reasons why the person in the dilemma should act in a certain way.

5. Test their own positions on a dilemma by:

    a. responding to the position of other people,

    b. presenting arguments for or against analogous dilemmas,

182

c. stating a position on a dilemma when circumstances change, and

d. stating a position and giving reasons for it from the point of view of another actor in the dilemma.

6. State a final position on the dilemma and state one or more reasons why that position is preferable to others.

3. How do you begin a discussion of a moral dilemma without it seeming contrived?

Prior to confronting students with a dilemma story, it is often helpful to use a warm-up strategy. An appropriate warm-up may help students to imagine the situation more clearly, to find the situation more interesting, or to see the relationship of the story to what they have been studying. Warm-up merely means introducing the story in a meaningful way rather than with a cold: "I want you to read this story and get ready to discuss it!"

For example, in the transcript, the teacher begins the class by asking the students if they can remember some of the important ideas from their examination of United States labor history. After several students respond, the teacher asks several warm-up questions to set the stage for the dilemma story:

— "How many of you know someone — a relative or a neighbor — who belongs to a labor union of some kind?"

— "How many of you know someone who has gone out on strike as part of a union protest?"

— "What is it like when someone is on strike?"

— "How do families get along when the husband or wife is not working?"

— "O.K., let's look at a story about a community where a lot of families have been on strike for over six weeks."

With *The Hospital Regulation*, you might use the following warm-up strategy:

— "How many of you have ever been in a hospital emergency room?"

— "What did you see?" (At this point, the teacher may make a list of observations on the chalkboard).

— "O.K., looking at our list, it appears as if an emergency room may be very boring or very crisis oriented. We have everything up here from 'taking out splinters' to 'heart attack victims.' Now I would like to share with you a true story about a nurse who spends a lot of time in the emergency room."

4. To be a successful teacher for moral reasoning, don't you need to analyze the student's level of reasoning?

No! The teaching process presented in this Handbook does not require teachers to become experts in identifying the stages of reasoning of their students. While teachers may associate general stage related remarks with particular stage reasoning, teachers should not attempt to categorize individual students at particular stages. First of all, a single comment will not reveal an individual's modal stage of reasoning. If teachers try to analyze a student's stage of reasoning based on single comments, they run the risk of categorizing the student incorrectly and negatively. Second, in any classroom there will be a variety of modal stages of moral reasoning. Therefore, the teaching strategy outlined in the Handbook emphasizes small group and large group discussions where students at adjacent stages of development confront one another and seriously discuss genuine social and moral problems. The teacher should set the atmosphere for such confrontation, promote the interaction, and maintain the focus on the moral issues. This is why teachers' skills in communication and group facilitation are more important to a productive discussion of a moral problem than their skill in stage interpretation. The teacher should not misuse his or her understanding of the theory to analyze the discussion and categorize students.

5. Are different students at different stages of moral development?

Most students are not at one specific stage of moral development. They move back and forth between two or three adjacent stages as they progress sequentially through the hierarchy of moral reasoning stages. In any given class, students generally represent a range of stages even though they may cluster around a common stage.

Generally students at ages 4-10 are at the pre-conventional level of moral reasoning while those at ages 11-16 are beginning to reason at the conventional level. Young adults move toward the post-conventional level. Research suggests that if children don't begin reasoning at Stage 4 by late adolescence, they can "freeze" at Stage 3 and never move beyond that stage, never achieve their full potential development.

6. Do the reasons a person gives for a moral decision represent a true stage or merely an articulation of something considered to be socially acceptable?

People can learn to parrot content cliches but they cannot actually comprehend reasoning much above their own level. An individual cannot consistently, over a period of time, parrot a level of reasoning which has not been internalized.

A stage of moral reasoning represents a way of looking at the world and understanding how it works. One cannot merely adopt a social or moral world view and consistently defend it without really understanding what it means.

7. Should teachers tell their students about the stages of moral reasoning as described by Kohlberg?

Students can be informed of the general nature of Kohlberg's theory of moral development. For the most meaningful results, this information can be shared with them after they have discussed several dilemmas. The teacher might ask: "How do you feel about dealing with these dilemma stories?" and follow the discussion elicited by this question with a brief and very general presentation of Kohlberg's description of the stages and sequence of moral reasoning.

Another way to accomplish this task is to talk to students about the development of individuals in terms of physical and intellectual development as well as moral development. Teachers can indicate that individuals change as they grow older. Changes occur in physical and intellectual development as one learns new things which expand one's capabilities. This developmental process also occurs in terms of one's moral viewpoints. As individuals develop morally, they learn to consider more points of view. Gradually their considerations move from thinking about just themselves to considerations of themselves, their immediate family and friends, to considerations about society in general. Indicate to students that discussing moral dilemmas may help them think about moral situations which they may face in their lifetime. This explanation of the theory of moral development should be geared to the age level and maturity of the students as well as to the course. For example, the explanation will certainly differ for a teacher of elementary children just as it may differ for a teacher of American History or a teacher of Psychology.

Teachers should be sure (1) to indicate that everyone goes through these stages in sequential fashion, (2) to stress that this idea is theoretical only, and (3) to explain that this theory is one way of explaining how people develop their thinking about moral issues. However, teachers should not peg students as being at a particular stage nor should teachers give the impression that they are evaluating students on a scale of stages. Students should never be graded on the teacher's perception of their movement through the stages.

8. How can you determine the level of a person's moral reasoning?

Kohlberg and his associates have developed a **moral judgment interview** which can determine an individual's modal stage of reasoning. The interviews are administered to students individually by trained interviewers. The moral judgment interview consists of three or four dilemma stories and a series of questions to which students respond in their own words. Each story in the interview includes a number of moral issues. The modal stage is determined by conducting a content analysis of the student responses. The scoring also involves a constant check for the consistency of reasoning across a number of related moral issues.

9. If teachers, like most adults, are only at Stages 3 or 4, how can they help kids develop beyond those stages?

Once again, the teaching strategy aims to get students talking to students without the constant intervention of the teacher so that the teacher's own stage will play little if any role in a discussion. The basic principle of this teaching process is to get students talking to one another about moral problems rather than talking or listening to teachers. Hence, the teacher functions primarily as a facilitator rather than as a director or indoctrinator.

10. What is the difference between the Teaching Plan and the Teaching Process?

The Teaching Plan includes the instructions for a particular dilemma story (alternative dilemmas and probe questions). Each dilemma should have a Teaching Plan which the teacher uses to prepare for a specific class discussion. The Teaching Process outlines the four steps or phases in a class discussion of a moral dilemma story. Although a teacher might refer to the step-by-step process during a discussion, it should be thought of as a general guide. We believe that each step and sub-step represent essential phases of a class discussion; however, the steps should not be considered a rigid format in the discussion of moral problems.

11. This teaching process seems to depend on a teacher's skill in asking appropriate questions. How do you know when to ask a question?

A common problem faced by many teachers in a moral dilemma discussion is a tendency to ask a sequence of questions without allowing students time to consider appropriate answers. This rapid fire questioning technique causes students to lose the continuity or theme of the discussion. This can be avoided by a minute of quiet after a probing type question. In addition, teachers should help students to focus on one aspect of the dilemma by asking a series of clarifying questions that relate to one particular issue. Teachers should avoid rapid shifts from one issue to another without providing appropriate transition.

Teachers in a moral dilemma discussion should also avoid conducting "interviews" with the individual students. Student "interviewing" occurs when the teacher asks a series of questions of one student and then moves on to another student and asks another series of questions. This pattern continues in a teacher-to-student sequence. If teachers find themselves questioning a series of students without any interaction between students, they should step back and evaluate the discussion. Additional students can be involved in the discussion by particular probe questions, perception checking questions, or questions about a student's evaluation of a previous student remark. Teachers should question individual students only when necessary to bring out the student's reasoning. At that point, the teacher should involve other students in the discussion.

12. The research related to the theory suggests that people need to listen to one another and exchange reasons during the discussion. What if students do not seem to be listening during a discussion?

Listening is a skill which does not receive enough attention in the classroom. The teacher's role in this entire process depends upon an ability to help students communicate effectively. One half of communication is listening. Therefore, we recommend a strong emphasis on listening skills. Certain interaction questions help students increase their listening skills:

"Would someone/you summarize the exchange of reasons you have just heard concerning why Sam should fill the order?"

"Could you tell me which part of Diana's comments you agree with and which part you object to?"

You might privately inform a particularly shy student or a non-involved student that you want him to be prepared to summarize some part of the next discussion. This way students are not threatened by your interest in their listening and questions are not used to accuse someone of not listening.

You should also encourage students to look at the person who is talking and try to make him feel that his comments are important. The way you arrange your class (chairs in a circle rather than rows) may have a lot to do with promoting student-to-student listening. Most importantly, your interest in student comments and your ability to keep the focus on the student speaker will demonstrate the significance of listening. Questions such as: "Would you tell us more about that?" and "I hadn't thought of it that way. Could you expand that idea for us a little?" help to focus on the student speaker. Your listening communicates more than you realize!

191

13. How closely is intelligence related to moral development?

It is possible to be highly intelligent yet not reason about moral problems at the post-conventional level. There is no concrete, one-to-one relationship between I.Q. and the stages of moral reasoning.

It is, however, more useful to think about the relationship of an individual's cognitive development and his or her moral development. Piaget's research indicates that during adolescence children generally move from Concrete Operations into Formal Operations. Formal operations, according to Piaget, represent the capacity to think about abstract concepts (logical consequences, implications, isolation of variables, and deductive hypothesis testing). The higher stages of moral reasoning are related to this kind of abstract thinking. Therefore, in order for someone to reason at the principled, post-conventional level of the moral development scale, he must also have formal operations capability. However, the capacity for abstract thinking **does not** guarantee reasoning at the higher stages of moral development.

A research study by Langer and Kuhn (1971) indicates that approximately 47 percent of all high school graduates are capable of formal operational thinking. Therefore, less than half of America's young adults are capable of moral reasoning above Stage 4.

14. How can you account for the discrepancy between what people really do in moral situations and the way they reason about what they should do?

Maturity of moral reasoning is a necessary but not sufficient cause for taking moral action. There is not a one-to-one relationship of moral reasoning to moral action. However, there are some data to indicate a relationship between mature moral development and principled behavior.

People may have completely different reasons for the same action. For example, with regard to the free speech movement at Berkeley, people at Stages 2 and 6 acted together, but for widely different reasons. The people at Stage 2 were involved for very self-centered reasons, yet they were ''mouthing'' the rhetoric of a higher stage, principled position. The people at Stage 6, however, were involved in the movement because they were acting out their commitment to certain principles of justice and human dignity. A specific type of action is not necessarily related to a particular stage of moral reasoning.

15. Do all moral dilemma discussions take a full class period?

Moral dilemma lessons can be taught in a number of time frames. In this Handbook, we have provided you with an example of a moral dilemma lesson geared to a 40-minute class period. Within the time frame of one class period, a moral dilemma lesson usually follows certain time guidelines. First, confronting a dilemma and stating a position on the dilemma story takes no longer than about 10 minutes of class time. Next, the discussion of reasoning accounts for approximately 25 minutes of class time. This testing of reasoning should be divided about equally between small and large class discussions. Finally, the remaining time in the period should be devoted to reflecting on a position and summarizing the various reasons brought out in the class discussion.

Moral dilemma lessons can also be organized over a number of class periods. In this case, the students might confront and state positions on a dilemma story during one class period and test their reasoning for 2 or 3 days and then spend a day reflecting on the discussions. A number of factors account for the need to extend moral dilemma discussions to more than one day. **First**, dilemmas produced by films, filmstrips, role-playing, or other more sophisticated methods take a longer period of time. **Second**, a particular dilemma may have a number of sub-dilemmas that need to be discussed. **Third**, during the testing stage the students may need to gather, analyze, and synthesize additional data relating to the dilemma story. Regardless of the length of the moral dilemma lesson, the final step in the process involves some kind of summarizing and reflecting activity. Most of the time of the moral dilemma lesson should be spent on the testing of reasoning with students interacting in small groups or in a full class discussion.

Some moral dilemma lessons may take only five to ten minutes. As students become involved in a continuous examination of issues in a systematic fashion, they will begin to identify moral issues and suggest them for discussion. A student may bring a newspaper editorial to class and ask if it represents a moral dilemma. At this time, a teacher may choose to spend five to ten minutes quickly identifying the moral issue and discussing the various implications for the characters involved. A similar discussion may evolve from a circumstance within the school or community. These spontaneous discussions of genuine social and moral problems represent the most natural kind of implementation of this approach. When students begin to identify moral issues which surround them and to initiate discussions of these issues, we have some reason to believe that moral development is occurring.

16. How can you redirect a discussion which gets off on some subject not related to the moral issues of the dilemma story?

In moral dilemma discussions, students have a tendency to discuss circumstances in the story that do not relate to the moral issues. For example, in *"Hey, Sam, The Truck Is Here,"* students may want to focus on the size of the truck and how much Sam will have to take from the store to fill the order when the truck arrives. A discussion or debate over the size of the truck while important in some respects is not central to the discussion of what Sam should do. Usually it is best to let the discussion continue for several minutes; the discussion may lead back to a moral issue without your intervention. However, if the students continue discussing the content of the dilemma and not the reasoning for assuming a particular position, the teacher should attempt to refocus the discussion on the moral issues in the story. This can be accomplished through a teacher probe question from the lesson plan. The teacher could relate the "content" diversion to the moral issue by picking up on the student's concern and rephrasing the discussion into a question focused on reasoning. For example, a teacher could ask a question such as, "How does the size of the truck relate to what Sam should do in this situation?" or "Suppose the truck is a big semi-tractor trailer. Should this influence Sam's decision? Why or why not?" Such questions require an answer which should work to return the focus to the issues of obligation, law, friendship, punishment, etc.

17. What happens to students who won't take a stand on a moral issue?

Undecided students are important to the teaching process. Students must not be made to feel that they must always decide on a particular issue. Ask them to listen and report on the reasons given in the small groups. Ask them to indicate near the end of the class which reason they could most agree with, and then ask them to suggest why they picked that particular reason. In this way, they are also thinking about their reasons.

18. Do teachers need to use the small group exercises as part of each discussion?

The small group strategies help students prepare for the larger discussion. Everyone has a better chance to share his opinions in the smaller groups. The primary goal is to get students talking to students about the moral problem. To meet this objective, the small group should ''prime'' the students for a lively exchange with the entire class. Occasionally, teachers choose to keep the entire class together as one large group to discuss the dilemma story. This often works well, but the deployment in smaller discussion groups places non-verbal students in a setting where they must participate in the discussion also. The majority of class time, however, should be spent in a large group discussion of the dilemma story.

19. The entire emphasis on the teacher's role as facilitator suggests that the teacher should not impose a position or an answer on the students. What if the students ask the teacher for his or her opinion?

Teachers should refrain from **introducing** their point of view. However, it is very natural for students to inquire about a teacher's position on the problem. After all, the teacher continues to ask them to take positions and defend them. If the question comes too early in the discussion and might influence some students, perhaps you can postpone commitment. Near the end of the discussion, however, the question may give the teacher an opportunity to summarize reasons given earlier and respond with an individual position and reason. The question may also provide a chance to suggest a reason which was not previously mentioned in the discussion. The question should come from the students, however. It will not create a climate of serious, open-minded inquiry if the students discover that the teacher gives the answer at the end of every discussion.

197

20. Should students ever be involved in evaluating the moral dilemma discussions?

At regular intervals, teachers should initiate a discussion with their students about their reactions to the moral dilemma discussions. Teachers might pose such questions as:

— ''Do you personally think that the discussions of moral dilemma stories are helpful in any way?''

— ''What have you gained from the discussions?''

— ''Do you think the discussions should be continued?''

— ''Do you think discussing social or moral issues makes any difference in how people deal with difficult problems?''

— ''What areas of the class discussions pose the most problems for you?''

21. If students are to continue thinking about social and moral issues, is there any neat way to close the discussion at the end of a class period?

Although consideration of moral issues should never really close, it is often helpful to use some kind of closing strategy to suggest that the discussion of a dilemma story or the consideration of a particular issue should continue beyond the classroom. An appropriate closing strategy may help students to continue to think about the moral issues.

For example, the teacher in the transcript asked the students to summarize some of the reasons which they had heard other students give during the discussion of *"Hey, Sam, The Truck Is Here."* The teacher also suggested to the students prior to their leaving the class that the discussion of the dilemma story would be related to a person who was to be a guest in class the next day. The teacher specifically stated that the students would have an opportunity to ask some other people about their views of the problem. Sometimes a closing strategy is nothing more than a specific suggestion to students to explore the story or the issues with someone outside the classroom, possibly parents, other students, or other teachers.

With *The Hospital Regulation*, you might use the following closing strategy:

Teacher:
Is there anyone in the class who knows someone who works in a hospital as a nurse, technician, or a doctor?

Several people raise their hands.

Teacher:
O.K., would it be possible for you to ask one of those individuals how they would respond to this dilemma story involving the nurse in the emergency room? This evening see if you can find out what they think. Tomorrow we will spend 5 or 10 minutes listening to your findings.

Or you could use this strategy:

Teacher:
How many of you think that this is a real problem in today's society?

Many of the students raise their hands.

Teacher:
Do you think you could relate this story to your parents? For instance, could you at the dinner table tonight tell your parents about this story involving the hospital regulation?

Many of the students indicate that they would like to do that.

Teacher:
Fine. Why don't you get your parents involved and find out their viewpoints on this particular moral problem? And we can spend some time tomorrow or the next day discussing other people's points of view on the same problem.

Closing strategies provide a means for suggesting that consideration of genuine moral problems goes beyond the classroom discussion. Teachers can create a variety of closing strategies which may serve to tie moral dilemma discussions into the curriculum context or will serve to promote continued discussion of moral issues with others in the community.

22. How do you deal with parents who question this approach to education?

Hopefully, parents will be interested in what you are doing in your classroom to discuss social and moral problems. Parents will probably be interested in learning that:

a. The teaching approach is based on Kohlberg's 15 years of research which indicates that all of us progress through stages of reasoning about social and moral problems. Some of us reach higher levels of moral maturity than others, and thinking about moral issues can be stimulated in the appropriate classroom setting.

b. The teaching process is not in any way an indoctrinating process or an inculcation of a set of values. It is a process designed to assist students in realizing their full potential for handling social and moral problems.

c. The process of discussing genuine social and moral problems is applicable beyond the classroom, for all ages, and in every aspect of family and community life. Therefore, parents might want to join a classroom discussion of a dilemma story. We would hope that classroom discussions of social or moral problems might lead to family discussion or discussions with a religious or community group. Serious consideration of issues like justice, life, and human dignity certainly belong in the home, but they should not be ignored in the school setting.

23. How does this approach compare to other values education strategies?

A complete answer to this question would require a very thorough examination of curriculum materials, teaching strategies, and supporting theories and assumptions. This particular approach is based on the assumption that indoctrination is not a productive technique for preparing young people to cope with social and moral problems. Leading classroom discussions of genuine moral problems moves beyond clarification strategies. Helping students to continually look for the best response to moral problems and encouraging them to analyze alternatives and to test their thinking moves beyond ethical relativity. The teaching process presented in this Handbook is certainly not the only approach for dealing with values questions; however, we believe it provides an exciting and systematic approach for helping students confront the many issues involving social or moral questions. For a more complete understanding of how this approach compares to other values education strategies, we recommend the following reading:

Superka, Douglas P., Patricia L. Johnson, Christine Ahrens. **Values Education: Approaches and Materials.** Social Science Education Consortium, Inc. (Boulder, Colorado: 1975).

Stewart, John S. "Clarifying Values Clarification: A Critique." **Phi Delta Kappan**, Volume LVI, #10, Pages 684-688. (June, 1975).

Stewart, John S. **Values Development Education**, 1973. Unpublished book available from the author at P.O. Box 12617, San Antonio, Texas 78212.

SELECTED
BIBLIOGRAPHY
OF
ADDITIONAL
SOURCES

READINGS RELATED TO THE THEORY

Beck, C.M. **Moral Education in the Schools: Some Practical Suggestions**. Toronto: The Ontario Institute for Studies in Education, 1971. Beck discusses the need to provide students with opportunities to confront moral problems and presents a plan for implementation within the curriculum.

Blatt, M. and L. Kohlberg. ''The Effects of Classroom Discussion on the Development of Moral Judgment.'' In L. Kohlberg and E. Turiel (Eds.), **Moralization: The Cognitive Developmental Approach**. New York: Holt, Rinehart, and Winston, in preparation.

Galbraith, R. and T. Jones. ''Teaching Strategies for Moral Dilemmas: An Application of Kohlberg's Theory of Moral Development to the Social Studies Classroom.'' In **Social Education**, January, 1975, Volume 39, Number 1, pages 16-22. The authors present a step-by-step teaching process for applying Kohlberg's understanding of moral reasoning in the classroom. The article includes a discussion of teaching skills and small group strategies which help to promote classroom dis-. cussions of social and moral problems.

Kohlberg, L. ''The Concepts of Developmental Psychology as the Central Guide to Education.'' In M. Reynolds (Ed.), **Psychology and the Process of Schooling in the Next Decade**. Minneapolis:

University of Minnesota Audio-Visual Extension, 1971.

Kohlberg, L. "Stages of Moral Development as the Basis for Moral Education." In C. Beck, E. Sullivan, and D. Crittendon (Eds.), **Moral Education**. Toronto: University of Toronto Press, 1971.

Kohlberg, L. **Collected Papers on Moral Development and Moral Education**. Cambridge: The Center for Moral Education, Harvard University, 1973. This single source provides a variety of articles written by Kohlberg and a number of associates. The articles focus primarily on a discussion of the theory.

CURRICULUM MATERIALS PRESENTING MORAL DILEMMAS

Elementary

Films:

Encyclopaedia Britannica Educational Corporation
425 North Michigan   Chicago, Illinois 60611
"Only Benjy Knows: Should He Tell?"
"Late for Dinner: Was Dawn Right?"
"The Lemonade Stand: What's Fair?"
"Who Needs Rules?"
"Where's Your Loyalty?"
"What's Your Authority?"

These films provide an excellent introduction to a moral dilemma story for elementary age children.

Filmstrips:

Guidance Associates, 757 Third Avenue,
New York, NY 10017

''First Things: Values'' — Three excellent sets of filmstrips, each including records or tapes, which focus on
specific moral issues. Each set also includes a teacher's
guide which briefly discusses the theory and how to
work with children in a discussion format.

Secondary
Films:

CRM-McGraw-Hill Films
1221 Avenue of the Americas, New York, NY 10020

''It's My Hobby'' — A great little film which features
the conflict between peer pressure and social
responsibility.

LCOA: Learning Corporation of America
1350 Avenue of the Americas, New York, NY 10019

''Trouble With the Law''
''Right to Live — Who Decides?''
''Politics, Power, and the Public Good''
''Love to Kill''
''Spaces Between People''

These films need to be previewed to determine which
·segment might be appropriate to introduce a dilemma
situation. They can provide an excellent source of
materials for class discussion.

OTHER CURRICULUM MATERIALS

Holt Social Studies Curriculum, Second Ed. (Edwin Fenton, General Editor). Each volume and each Teacher's Guide includes a series of dilemma stories which fit within the flow of the curriculum. (Holt, Rinehart & Winston, Inc.)

Choices: Situations to Stimulate Thought and Expression by Thelma Altshuler. Prentice-Hall, 1970. This source provides a variety of potential dilemma situations which might be adapted for use in a classroom.

Photo Study Cards, Bender, David and McCuen, Gary. (Classroom discussion kits on moral and social problems.) Greenhaven Press, Inc., Box 831, Anoka, Minnesota 55303.

>   Kit 1: Who Are You?
>   Kit 2: Who Would You Like To Be?
>   Kit 3: What Do You Value?
>   Kit 4: You and Authority
>   Kit 5: You and Social Responsibility

Ron Galbraith received his B.A. and M.A. in History from Ball State University and is currently completing a Doctor of Arts in History at Carnegie-Mellon University. He taught History at Ball State University (1970-1972) and at Carnegie-Mellon University (1973). He participated as a Staff Associate on the Harvard/Carnegie-Mellon Values Education Project and served as Director of the Responsible Citizenship Project in Pittsburgh. Mr. Galbraith designs and uses curriculum materials with both elementary and secondary students. He currently consults with various school districts concerned with teaching methods, values education, and curriculum development. He has directed many workshops, some sponsored by the National Council for the Social Studies, where the methods and strategies presented in this handbook were applied and tested.

Thomas M. Jones received his B.A. in History and his M.A. in Education from the University of Rochester. He has completed his course work for a Doctor of Arts in History at Carnegie-Mellon University. He participated as a Staff Associate on the Harvard/Carnegie-Mellon Values Education Project and has served as a consultant to various school systems and professional organizations dealing with inquiry and values education. He is currently teaching secondary social studies at Irondequoit High School in Rochester, New York. He has directed and participated in many workshops, some sponsored by the National Council for the Social Studies, where the methods and strategies presented in this handbook were applied and tested.

DATE DUE

Fac 11/1/82			
NOV 2 8 1983			
NOV 1 2 1984			
FAC			
OCT 2 8 1985			